A GENEALOGIST'S REFRESHER COURSE

SECOND EDITION

By
Judy Jacobson

CLEARFIELD

Printed for
Clearfield Company, Inc. by
Genealogical Publishing Co., Inc.
Baltimore, Maryland
1996

Reprinted for
Clearfield Company, Inc. by
Genealogical Publishing Co., Inc.
Baltimore, Maryland
2004

International Standard Book Number: 0-8063-4627-2

Made in the United States of America

Table of Contents

Fables and endless
genealogies.
- 1 Timothy
Bible

Before We Go Any Further

I've seen the usual "How-to" books for genealogists. Some lead you step-by-step through the beginnings of a family research project. Some list addresses of all the places to write or to go to in order to find information. Some include forms on which you are supposed to write all the information you collect. Some tell you how to publish what you find.

But that is not what this book is about.

After my children were born, I began researching my family, and then my husband's. Then I started corresponding with others researching the same families. People started to contact me about families from our county, even though I had no familial relationship to them. That took up so much of my time, I finally decided to charge for my services. My home business expanded until my research area covered all the surrounding counties and into the next state. Eventually all the information I had accumulated, with a little additional research, turned into several published books.

In the meantime, I was working as a librarian, first in a public library and then at a university library. And I was seeing a lot of family historians, both professional and amateur, going through.

After deciding to take an early "retirement" to spend more time with my family, I became a member of the board of trustees, then a guide, and finally a semi-official curator for our local historical museum. And again, I saw genealogists coming through, hoping to find that elusive clue they needed to put it all together.

Through it all - the research, the libraries, and the museum - I began to discover common mistakes family historians made. I uncovered places genealogists should have been

checking for information, but hadn't been. And I decided to
pass those little bits and pieces of advice on to you.

That is what this book is about.

If men could learn
from history,
What lessons it
might teach us!
-Samuel
Coleridge

1

Why Climb Your Family Tree

The present becomes the past and ceases to exist unless it has been recorded. The past is important, but it disappears quickly.

When I had children of my own, I wanted to give them a past to help them understand their present and future. A great-aunt gave me the family Bible and some aged pictures, while my mother dug out the long saved papers and retold the tales I'd never really listened to before. I went after all the historical evidence I could find like a woman possessed.

As a mystery buff, I look at the process as a master whodunit, with one clue leading to another. Churchill might call it "a riddle wrapped in a mystery." It is also a genetics, geography and history lesson all rolled into one. It is an ego-inflator and ego-deflator. It may be a type of self-analysis or an interesting pastime.

There can be as many reasons for conducting a genealogical search as there are researchers. Some start the climb as part of their religious convictions. A number of years ago, some people began after seeing the television mini series or reading Alex Haley's *Roots*. They too wanted to know their origins. With today's families spread all over the country; some are looking for a center - a home. Those from more dysfunctional families are looking for something to bring some balance into their lives. And others, like me, began when they first became parents or grandparents. They wanted to pass on their heritage. And still others felt the need to find someone "important" in their background.

Today genealogy searches have taken on a new look. Medical breakthroughs and a new understanding of hereditary diseases have led a number of families to trace their medical ancestry.

But whatever your reasons, don't expect to scale your family tree in one month or even six: it is not an easy climb. Each generation back doubles in size. You have two parents, four grandparents, eight great-grandparents, and so forth. Twenty generations give you more than one million ancestors who were born; married, usually; produced off-spring, sometimes excessively; worried about homes, bills and health; and died.

We must never assume
that which is
incapable of proof.
-G.H. Lewis
*The Physiology
of Common Life*

2

Circumstantial Evidence

In order to build, you need the names, dates and places of the BASIC IMPORTANT EVENTS of a person's life; such as his birth, marriage and death dates. Other information, like the occupation of a person is supplemental information which you might find interesting; but can not be considered one of the basics.

When searching for this information you might uncover two different birth dates or other conflicting information for the same person. Then you have to look at the authenticity of the material you are using.

It is important to keep in mind that there are several types of evidence. PRIMARY SOURCE evidence or "best evidence" would be an eyewitness to an event, was concerned with it and/or recorded it immediately. A mother would know her child's name and birth place and date. But Aunt Edna, who heard about the new family member from Grandma Miller, should not be considered a primary source of evidence. Aunt Edna was not an eyewitness, was not directly concerned with it and did not record it immediately, if at all.

But the primary source varies depending upon the document or event. In governmental records, any information which does not apply directly to that record, is considered a SECONDARY SOURCE evidence. Today we might call it "second-hand" or "hearsay" information. On a death certificate, for instance, the date and cause of death would be considered primary information. The doctor filling out the certificate would meet all the criteria as a primary source of evidence for that information. However, the doctor could not be considered the primary source for information such as date and place of birth and parents' names. Even if the widow or child had provided

3

the information for the death certificate; the information might still have been wrong. The spouse or child might never have known their husband's or father's mother's maiden name. And if, at one time, they knew the information needed, it could have been forgotten in the grief of losing a loved one or the years since first hearing the information from someone else.

It wasn't until he got his birth certificate for the army that my father discovered that his birth date and legal name were not what his parents had always told him. Although he had been told he had a middle name, none appeared on the certificate. And his parents had been celebrating his birthday a week early - on his sister's birth date. So in this case, even a primary source (his mother was definitely concerned with his birth) can be mistaken.

Keep in mind which document is being used to determine which information is probably primary and which is probably secondary.

	Considered a	
	Primary Source	Secondary Source
Birth Certificate	date of birth place of birth name of mother name of child	father's name address of mother

Marriage License	date of marriage
	place of marriage
	name of couple
		names of
		    couple's
		    parents

Death Certificate	date of death cause of death place of death name of deceased name of spouse	age at death date of birth names of parents years lived at address place of birth

And of course, courtroom testimony to which everything is testified under oath should be a primary source. But even then, people testify as to what they believe to be true. Two people can witness the same event, and yet describe it completely differently.

The final type of evidence it INDIRECT or "circumstantial." This is evidence determined by reason.

For instance, in 1850, Sarah Blalock married Leonard Clark in Ypsilanti, Michigan. The 1850 and 1860 censuses showed Sarah was born in New York circa 1830. A John and Esther Blalock, born circa 1808 and 1810 respectively, were the only Blalocks living in the same county in 1850. Their eldest child living at home was James Blalock, born circa 1832 in New York.

So there was indirect evidence that Sarah could have been the daughter of John and Esther Blalock. When it was discovered that the parents of John Blalock were named James and Sarah, the indirect evidence grew.

SUPPLEMENTAL INFORMATION is perhaps the most fun. That is the extraneous information learned about the individual. Basic important events; like names, dates and places; are not part of supplemental information. However, supplemental information can give clues about the basic important events. While military service is a supplemental event, military records can sometimes lead to information about place of residence, marriages, children and date of death.

I've always thought that those genealogists who keep searching only for the basic important events are missing something. The fact that Great-great-great grandpa William Smith helped build the Erie Canal is interesting. And finding that ancestor Daniel Lander was hanged for his service with pirate Thomas Pound is fascinating. Who doesn't like to think some of the swashbuckling personality is hidden deep inside themselves?

But as important as the source is, the CREDIBILITY of the evidence must also be taken into consideration. Don't have blind faith in those stories handed down through the family. Elements of the story could have been left out or misunderstood as it was passed from person to person. The woman that Grandma was taught to call "Aunt Mabel" as a child may have had no family relationsip to her at all.

There are questions to ask. How long was it between the occurrence of the event and the recording? Even a primary source might forget details, if too much time has elapsed.

Was the material translated from its original source? If so, how familiar was the translator with the original language? Is the translation credible?

Was the original document altered in any way? Was the use of different inks obvious? Were there erasures or crossed out words?

Was this an edited version of an original? Was it an extract in which a direct quotation was made more concise by eliminating series of words and replacing them with a series of three dots? Was the original paraphrased? In other words, did an editor interpret the original for himself? If so, did the interpretation maintain the integrity of the piece?

Little one! Little
one!
I am searching
everywhere.
               -James
               Stephens
               The Snail

3

Searching Everywhere

The very first thing anyone beginning a genealogy search
should do is find out if anyone else has already researched
the line. Relatives may know. If they don't, check in
Genealogical and Local History Books in Print and *Family
Histories in the Library of Congress.*

Frequently the best clues for beginning a genealogical
search are sitting right in your own HOME. Some which might be
found in the your home or homes of relatives include -

Account books/ledgers
Address books
Adoption papers
Anniversary announcements
Appointment books
Apprentice records
Autograph albums
Awards
Baby books
Bank books
Bank statements
Baptismal certificates
Beneficiary records
Bills of sale
Bills
Bounty papers
Business licenses
Check stubs
College degrees
Confirmation
Contracts
Deeds

Diaries/journals
Disability records
Discharge papers
Divorce papers
Driver's licence
Engagement announcements
Family Bible
Family traditions
Financial records
Funeral memorial cards
Genealogies
Graduation announcements
Greeting cards
Guardian papers
Health records
High school diplomas
Hometown newspapers
I.D. card
Insurance policies
Land grants
Leases
Letters

Local histories	Report cards
Marriage licenses	School yearbooks
Medals	School records
Military uniforms	Scrapbooks
Mortgages	Social Security card
Naturalization papers	Subpoenas
New home announcements	Summons
Newspaper clippings	Tax notice
Obituaries	Tax records
Ordination certificates	Uniforms
Passports	Videos
Photograph albums	Water rights
Postcards	Wedding guest book
Prescription bottles	Wedding invitations
Professional licenses	Wills

Other FAMILY MEMBERS, especially older relatives - parents, grandparents, aunts - may have the family Bible, old letters, pictures, newspaper clippings and, most importantly, memories to aid your research. Your ancestors often kept better records than you think.

While other details might prove to be of interest, the chief items that need to be extracted from these sources are names, dates, places and relationships. Land and baptismal records; birth, marriage and death certificates; and wills and other probate records often give all or some of the information that can lead to the next generation.

For example, a child's birth certificate lists the place and date of birth and the parents' names. That gives a place and time frame in which to search for the parents' marriage license.

When interviewing an elderly relative, have previously prepared questions to keep you on track. Relatives may ramble, but if you keep a chart with you, you can write down only the essential information. But take along some extra paper. Some of those ramblings may prove worthy of being written down. Patience is important.

Tape record or, better yet, video tape the elderly members of the family, telling their stories. Those records can be referred to even after the older person has died. And the tapes can become treasured heirlooms for you children and grandchildren.

Elderly family members also can guide you to family burial places, possibly containing several generations. CEMETERY AND BURIAL RECORDS and TOMBSTONE INSCRIPTIONS can

provide you with an amazing amount of information about your
ancestors. For instance, a marker in Southold, Long island
read

HERE

LIETH THE BODY

OF HANNAH GRIFFING

WIFE OF JASPER

GRIFFING BORN AT

MANCHESTER IN NEW

ENGLAND AGED 46 YEARS

AND 8 DAYES AND WAS

MOTHER OF 14 CHILDREN

AND DEPARTED THIS LIFE

IN SOVTHOLD THE 20

DAY OF APRIL 1699

The tombstone gave the place and date of birth and death.
In addition, a genealogist determined Hannah's husband's name
and the number of children she had. Her parents might be found
by looking in Southold or Manchester. Her parents obviously
emigrated before Hannah's 1653 birth. Did Jasper's will list
the names of Hannah's children?

County, village, city, and township GOVERNMENTAL RECORDS
yield marriage license applications, probate records, land
deeds, and birth and death certificates. This is one of the
most widely used genealogical tools.

Keep in mind that in some states, VITAL RECORDS, such as
birth, death, marriage and divorce records are kept in the
state division of vital statistics, while in other states they
are kept in the appropriate county courthouse.

There are a variety of other LOCAL SOURCES. Newspaper
morgues have obituaries; churches keep baptismal, marriage and
funeral records; and libraries preserve family and local
histories. Telephone and city directories can lead to unknown
cousins with clues, old photographs or family Bibles.

University and local public LIBRARIES offer a variety of
categories of books of use to the genealogist. Included are
local books, like cemetery records and historical sketches;
state books, like marriages in other counties and census
records; regional books, like pioneers and taxpayers of
neighboring counties; and family histories. A number of "how
to" books give directions of how to organize a genealogy
search and list places to go for information.

Some public and university libraries have extensive
genealogy and history sections. You can not assume that only

genealogy type books will yield valuable research information. Books like *History of Long Island* contain a great many references to early settlers and is found among history books in the library.

The MILITARY SERVICE RECORDS of the National Archives has information on veterans of all American wars from the American Revolution through the Spanish-American War. University libraries, county courthouses and state archives all may have additional military and, in particular, Civil War records including pension applications. The Chamber of Commerce or the public library might be able to supply you with the names and addresses of the local levels of organizations, such as Daughters of the Confederacy and Daughters of the American Revolution, which might provide information concerning area soldiers in those wars.

At the NATIONAL LEVEL, the Library of Congress and the National Archives & Record Service in Washington, D.C. are among the best genealogical sources in the United States. But since records are kept by year in most cases, you need to know the approximate date of the event for which you are looking.

The federal census from 1790 to 1840 listed only the head of the house, with the numbers of males and females in each age category included. However, beginning with 1850, the age, place of birth and occupation of everyone in the household was listed. The first U.S. census was taken in 1790. Most of the 1890 census records are either damaged or missing. Many large university libraries have their region's censuses on microfilm, keep indexes and supply copiers for them.

Expensive trips are not necessary in order to do a good genealogy search. Census records can be rented and sent to your public library through the MAIL.

Correspondence with relatives, libraries and government officials can accomplish a great deal. However, in order to get specific answers, ask specific questions. Letters that are too long, too vague, or that do not include a self-addressed envelope will be thrown away. Letters reading "Send me everything you know about Grandpa Andrews" will not be answered. Don't expect too much of other people. They don't care about your research like you do. If you want them to do you a favor, you need to make it easy for them to do it.

I've been drunk for about
a week now and I thought it
might sober me up to sit in
the library.
    -F. Scott Fitzgerald
    The Great Gatsby

4

Circulating Around the Library

Before visiting the library, develop a good portable
filing system for carrying your basic information.
Organization is terribly important. The more information you
have with you, the less time you will spend researching the
wrong family. I use a small metal file case with three by five
cards filed alphabetically by family name. It will also save
you from copying unneeded materials. Considering that many
libraries charge twenty-five cents a copy and courthouses
charging up to fifty cents a copy, that can add up to a fair
amount of money.

A number of genealogists use lap top or notebook
computers allowing new information to be added immediately and
old information checked instantaneously.

GENEALOGY SOURCE BOOKS include the "how-to's" like *How to
Find Your Family Roots* by Bear and Demong and the "where-to-
go's" like *Genealogical Libraries Within 300 Miles of
Starkville* by the Oktibbeha County Historical and Genealogical
Society. Guides to materials in state archives like North
Carolina's multi-volumed edition are frequently available. In
addition, the subject index for *Books in Print* and
Genealogical and Local History Books in Print lead to
additional sources and provide purchasing information.

Most genealogists are aware of the information available
in the local history or genealogical sections of the library.
And while the family histories; local, state, national, and
international genealogical information books; and National
Society of Daughters of Founders and Patriots of America and
Daughters of the American Revolution lineage books are very
important to a search; there is an abundance of information
outside of the genealogy collection, in the GENERAL

11

COLLECTION. Gifts of information can be found in a library's sociology, history, geography, biography, and reference sections. After discovering ancestors of mine were also the grandparents of Benjamin Franklin, I found my ancestors in history books and biographies of Franklin, including delightful descriptions of my ancestors in Franklin's own words.

Encyclopedic or dictionary style biographies, like the various *Who's Who*, give useful information. Numerous books have been printed featuring sketches of important persons in the early development of an area, a state, a region, or even the nation.

History books led me to another ancestor, a pirate named Daniel Landers. Law books gave a description of his trial for piracy and his sentence of hanging.

Other history books, like *A Sweet and Alien Land* by the van der Zees and *Ghost Towns of Colorado* by Brown are potential sources. Historical books provide information, like John Youngs was one of the first settlers of Southold, Long Island.

Histories of schools or school systems might sound dreary, but they are the stories of proud pioneers interested in improving their children's chances for success.

For instance, in *A History of the Romeo Community School District 1824-1976*, Elizabeth Kane takes Macomb County, Michigan from the days of one-room schoolhouses into a modern school system and includes a pictorial history. Rolls of students, lists of faculty members, programs for school plays and identified pictures of sports teams give a Macomb County researcher a great deal of useful information. Most Macomb kids went through those schools.

On the college level, old yearbooks and university records give a great deal of information concerning former students. Many alumni associations, especially on the college level, have compiled biographies of former students.

Local directories in a variety of formats are usually saved by libraries and are of definite use to genealogists.
  -Telephone books usually contain names, modified addresses, and telephone numbers.
  -City directories, in addition to the usual telephone directory information, may give place of employment, name of spouse and number of people living at the address.

-Reverse or crisscross directories list by address and by telephone.

Sociology books, such as *Voyagers to the West* by Boulin and *Island of Hope, Island of Tears* by Brownstone, Franck, and Brownstone, give insight into lives of people of the time. Books like *Highland Clans and Tartans* by Munro, *Special Collections in Libraries in the Southeast* edited by Howell, and reference gazetteers and atlases are all books in a library's general collection which can provide significant material for the genealogist.

While most librarians are not specifically trained in genealogy, their chief skill is knowing where to find answers. Although the public's confidence in the librarian is gratifying, some genealogists have exaggerated views of what the librarians can and should do. They are not travel agents (Where is a good place to stay while I am in town?). Neither are they babysitters for your children while you lose yourself in your research, nor are they counselors.

Because of budget limitations, staff sizes are usually limited and librarians find themselves with too much to do and too little time in which to do it. A librarian should only be expected to direct researchers to the relevant areas of the library, but the work must be yours.

Do not expect libraries to lend reference, genealogy or local history books. If they will not lend them to their own local patrons who pay the taxes that support the library, they certainly will not lend to outsiders.

Many of the books most useful to the genealogist are expensive, rare, or delicate. Often local history books are limited editions or out-of-print, meaning they cannot be replaced if lost. And because of the delicate condition, a lot of handling of these rare item could be harmful to them.

However, it does occasionally happen that a library will loan a genealogy or local history book. One patron wanted to see a rare county history so badly, she placed a call to the library owning the book and offered to send a hefty deposit to pay shipping cost, and agreed to use the book only in her local library. The lending library sent the book INTERLIBRARY LOAN as soon as the deposit arrived.

"How-to" books are easier to borrow through interlibrary loan. Yet, books like De Platt's *Genealogical Historical Guide to Latin America*, Stewart's *Liberia Genealogical Research*, Baywater's *Greek Genealogical Research*, Low's *China*

Connection: Finding Ancestral Roots for Chinese in America, and Szalasznyj's *How to Research Your Ukranian Ancestry in Saskatchewan* can make difficult searches easier.

Another option is borrowing from the state library commission. Usually, a cooperative has been set-up between most public libraries and their state's library commission. While other public libraries in the state will generally not lend genealogy books on interlibrary loan, the state library commission is much more willing to lend the book, if they own it. Frequently limitations are put on the loan, such as the book can not leave the borrowing library.

To find what libraries own a specific book, ask your local librarian for a listing of libraries owning it. There should be an interlibrary loan librarian in all library systems, no matter how small. They have available to them microfiche and computer network systems which allow libraries to locate a book, sometimes within minutes.

When the list of holding libraries arrives, check for the closest. Is it near enough to visit? If not, ask your librarian to try to borrow it. If the holding library rejects the request, write them asking them to photocopy pages applying to your family. Librarians are willing to copy appropriate pages as long as the request conforms with federal copyright laws. So do not expect them to photocopy the entire book. It would probably be illegal and definitely too time-consuming for the librarian.

Photocopying costs can range from 10 to 50 cents per copy. Depending upon how many pages are sent, postage could add up to another $1.50. Libraries are financed by their local patrons through their taxes; not by you. Do not expect "freebies".

So whenever writing any library for help, always enclose a check for $2.00 to $5.00 to cover postage and copying charges. It also might be appropriate to tell the library to keep any leftover funds as a donation to the library.

Since most librarians have little genealogy training; do not be surprised if your letter is answered half-heartedly, pushed off onto an underling, or thrown-away. But do not give up hope. Most librarians try to help as best as they can. Local genealogists sometimes help libraries with genealogy questions. And sometimes, just sometimes, you will find a small town library with an excellent genealogical section manned by a local history expert.

14

When writing to a library, include only specifics - what you have and what you need. Librarians do not care how long or why you have been searching. QUERIES that are long, vague, or do not include at least a self-addressed stamped envelope may get thrown away. Letters reading "Send me everything you have on the Smith family" may not get answered. The letter is too vague, and the librarian cannot clarify questions. Answering them could be wasting the librarian's time.

Type or write the letter in your neatest handwriting. The librarian must be able to read your questions in order to answer them.

If you publish your information, even as a limited edition, donate a copy to your local library. Gifts such as this are always welcome and a nice way to thank a library for their help.

Specialty libraries; like Hawaii's Mission Children's Society Library, Stanford University's Chicano Reference Library and Bluffton, Ohio's Mennonite Historical Library; are concerned with groups of people and frequently hold sources not readily available elsewhere. Other specialty libraries, like Michigan's Bentley Historical Library, are devoted to documenting the history of an area.

Large university libraries are another excellent source of information. In the stacks are histories of areas across the United States and around the world. Their local history and genealogical area (frequently a part of "Special Collections") usually holds a large collection of state and regional sources. Often, university libraries have combined indexes for a number of journal. Many hold federal censuses and indexes, and civil war records on MICROFILM.

University ARCHIVES collect and catalogue and preserve papers of well-known, and sometimes not so well-known, early citizens of the state. Other archives can be found on the state level and at other institutions, such as the Presbyterian Church Archives.

I asked several librarians how they felt about genealogy researchers. While most comments were positive, there also were negative remarks, such as -

"Genealogists expect us to know and have everything. They think we should have all census records. Don't they understand the cost involved? We have a limited budget."

"Genealogists underline in books, turn down page corners, and spread their MacDonald's lunches all over our tables, completely ignoring out 'No Food or Drink' signs."

"They corner us and tell us about their genealogy - who was at the family reunion, what was in grandpa's will. Don't they realize we have jobs that need to be done and other patrons that need to be served?"

"A genealogist will use anything - a candy wrapper, match, ice cream stick, or bobby pin - as a bookmark."

But when I reported these comments to some family historians, they were fierce in their disagreement. They were sure that librarians were interested when they talked about their family trees. It never entered their minds that the librarians might have just been being polite.

Other researchers swore that they would never mark in books or eat in the library. And I agree. But while the librarians' comments do not apply to all genealogists, there are enough that are so caught up in their research that they just forget their manners.

Remember, the librarian can be your most important resource in your search for your ancestors. But to be successful, keep in mind what a librarian can do and that libraries have other patrons too.

Histories make men
wise.

-Bacon
Of Studies

5

Second-Hand Rose

Whether it is a volume of the 1937 *Compendium of American Genealogy* or *Historical Sketches of Oktibbeha County*, you might find a useful book for sale in a second-hand book store or a genealogical magazine want ad, and discover your ancestors listed in them. And while family histories are of little interest to most people, the right family history or local history might be of extraordinary interest to you.

One book entitled *A Journal Comprising an Account of the Loss of the Brig. Commerce of Hartford (Con.) James Riley, Master, Upon the Western Coast of Africa, August 28th, 1815; Also of Slavery and Sufferings of the Author and the Rest of the Crew, upon the Desert of Zahara, in the years 1815, 1816, 1817; with Accounts of the Manners, Customs and Habits of Wandering Arabs; Also a Brief Historical and Geneagraphical View of the Continent of Africa* by Archibald Robbin has a mouthful of a title. But this slim book also holds genealogical information about Robbins and his shipmates and was found in a used bookstore.

Another second-hand book, *As I Remember It: Stories of Civil War Times* By B.C. Harpole, includes some genealogical information in the introduction. The book itself recounts life in a rural area of the South during and just following the Civil War, including events directly affecting the author's family and their friends.

A copy of *The Territorial Papers of the United States: The Territory of Michigan 1805-1820* is just one of a series of collections of records for parts of the United States which were territories at one time. These territorial papers include letters written to and from government officials conferring property, making appointments , answering complaints, commanding troops and generally running the territorial government. Many early settlers are named.

Occasionally even a family Bible; complete with a family's birth, death and marriage dates; can be found. Sometimes a genealogist will pick-up such a "find" even when their own families are not mentioned, and will attempt to get the Bible into the hands of a genealogist whose families are mentioned.

While used book stores are a good source - especially ones in bigger cities; those are more of a "hit and miss" when trying to find a specific book and are seldom successful. A better source for specific second-hand books are genealogical magazines. Some of these publications have a classified ad section in which readers can advertize for publications they want to purchase and publications they wish to sell.

And if his name be
George,
I'll call him Peter.
-Shakespeare
King John

5

What's in a Name?

Bertoit Brecht wrote "A name is an uncertain thing. You can't count on it." How right Brecht was! You would expect finding a name would be the easiest part of ancestor hunting. But, as Brecht said, "A name is an uncertain thing."

Most male names of New England settlers were either Anglo-Saxon or Norman origin. Of the 452 free Englishmen in Boston between 1630 and 1634 the six most frequent names - John, William, Thomas, Richard, Robert, and Edward - were of Norman origin, with little religious connotation. But ninety percent of the children of those same freedmen were given Biblical names. Between 1630 and 1670, twenty-one percent of the women born in the Massachusetts Bay Colony were named Mary, seventeen percent were Elizabeth, and fifteen percent were Sarah. Middle names for both men and women were not frequently given before 1731. But they had become quite common by 1785.

When an ancestor originated in a foreign country, the names could appear in records in either the original or the translated English form. Keep in mind what kind of record you are using. For instance, a French or French-Canadian record would probably have the French version of the name. But after immigrating, English or American versions might appear in English or American documents. An example of some interchangeable English and French names are -

Andrew	Andre
John	Jean
Anthony	Antoine
Stephen	Etienne
Mary	Marie
Lawrence	Laurant / Eustache
William	Guillaume

19

The name in the family Bible may not agree with the tombstone. Either may have been written or carved years after the persons death. A distraught widow may have never met her husband's parents, but was expected to fill out information about them on his death certificate.

Jenny might be listed as Johnny on a census record. John Smythe might appear as John Smith. The census taker might have misunderstood the name, written sloppily, spelled poorly or written phonetically. Old style handwriting added to the problem when "s" appeared as "f" and "u" appeared as "v".

Probably the hardest part of genealogy research is keeping FIRST NAMES straight. Names change. Eugene Fields, in "Jest 'Fore Christmas" clearly demonstrated part of the problem:

> Father calls me William,
> Sister calls me Will,
> Mother calls me Willie,
> But the fellers call me Bill.

Someone might be referred to as Bill in one census and Willie in another. Bertha could be called "Birdie", "Bert" or "Bertie;" Cornelia could be known as "Corny," "Nelle" or "Nelly;"and Margaret could be called "Daisy." "Diah" might have been named Jedediah, Obadiah or Zedidiah. "Ossy" or "Ozzy" could have legally been an Oscar, Oswald or Osmond.

John and Christopher Youngs were sons of Christopher Youngs, Sr. Each of the sons named one of their sons Christopher. Four Christopher Youngs resided in the same small town, at the same time. To a genealogist working one to two hundred years later, it can be mighty confusing.

In Center Grove, Mississippi, there are two tombstones for the wife of Squire Harpole.

Susan	Susana Harpole
wife of Squire	wife of Squire
Harpole	Harpole
b. Mar 3, 1814	b. Mar 3, 1814
d. March 28, 1877	in Georgia
	d. March 28, 1877
	in Oktibbeha Co.

Since the dates and husband's name are the same, both stones must be for the same person. However, the first name is different. The one on the left was probably erected shortly after Susan died. The one on the right was erected in 1961 by descendants of Squire Harpole and his wife. The information on the one on the right must be considered secondary information.

In addition, for a variety of reasons, families have altered or completely changed the spelling of their SURNAMES. Many were simplified or Americanized when someone immigrated to the United States. The German name "Scwartz" might have been translated and have become "Black". The French "Blanc" may have become "White". The Spanish "Carnicero" may have become "Butcher." The Polish "Lis" may have become "Fox."

Many Europeans arrived in the New World with two surnames; like James Smythe-Gordon, Jean Morin du Loudun or James Erskine, Earl of Mar. Several reasons for the double surnames were
- Some owners took the titles of their estates as their second name. And frequently the estate title was the one that survived as the single family name instead of the original family name.
- The name, or double name, of a wife sometimes was joined to the husband's. For instance, Godet dit Marentette name came about when Jacques Godet married Margaret Duquay dit Marentette.
- Sometimes a second name was given to distinguish one family from another family with the same surname.
- Some glorified the section of the country they came from by adding the name of the province, city, or town to their name. Literally, Jean Morin du Loudun meant Jean Morin of the town of Loudun.
- Sometimes the second name originated from the peculiar circumstances of a person's birth. For instance, Nicholas Campau dit Niagara was born at the Niagara Falls portage.
Upon reaching the New World, the name might be shortened. So Jean Morin du Loudun might have become John Morin, John Loudun, or even John Landon.

Those of Spanish heritage usually also have two or more surnames. The first is the father's first surname: the second is the mother's first surname. Depending upon the era, one surname could have been either the father's first or second surname and the other either of the mother's. Or both surnames could been the father's.

Upon marriage, the Spanish woman would not take her husband's name. If Xavier Domingo Franco had married Maria Perez Delgado, the wife would have become either Sra. Maria Perez Delgado or Maria Perez Delgado de Domingo.

In Scandinavia, a person's surname was derived from his father's first name. For instance, Peder Ingbritsen was the father of Jakob Pedersen (son of Peder). Jakob's son became Albert Jakobsen. However, when Albert Jakobsen arrived in the United States, he decided to Americanize his last name and became Albert Jacobson. All of Albert's children, since they were born in the United States became Jacobsons, even though their paternal great-grandfather was an Ingbritsen.

Probably because of the Scandinavian influence, Icelandic children have been named the same way. Halldora Kristiansdottir was the daughter of Kristian. Her brother's last name was Kristiansen.

Along the same lines, years ago, Robert ap David was the son of David in Wales, but might have become Robert David, Davis or Davies in America. "Ap" in Wales, "Fitz" in Ireland, "wicz" in Poland, and "ez" in Spain all meant "son of" when added to a name.

MacDonald was the son of Donald in Scotland. Actually the prefixes Mac / Mc / M' were added with no consistency. If a proper name followed "Mac", as in MacDonald, the name was capitalized. If not, the second name was in lower case, as in "Maclean." And, before the 1600's, no surnames were used at all in Scotland.

In addition, spellings varied: Landon could appear as "Landers", "Lankton", or "Langdon". "Conklin" could appear as "Conkling": Patterson" might show up as "Pattinson".

Surprisingly, the U.S. Central Intelligence Agency has produced a number of books of foreign names, including *Czech Personal Names* and *Armenian Personal Names*. Other useful books include Peters *Mennotische Namen* (Mennonite Names), Chapuy's *Origine des Noms Patroymiques Francais* (Origins of French Family Names), Kaganoff's *A Dictionary of Jewish Names and Their History*, and West's *An Atlas of Louisiana Surnames of French and Spanish Origin*. In addition, the American Names Society publishes an helpful journal.

The New England "Mr." was a TITLE applied to sea captains, members of the military, school masters, distinguished merchants, physicians, judges, clergymen, and freemen with two college degrees. Any female in their family was referred to as "Mrs." Those of a lesser status were referred to as "Goodman" or "Goodwife."

A "Squire" was originally a member of the British gentry ranking below knight, but above gentleman. As years were by, the title was given to an owner of a country estate, usually the principal landowner in the area. That title migrated to the New World with British emigrants.

"Seigneur" was the French version of "Squire" awarded to the "lord of the manor." "Monsieur" originated with the word "Sieur" which was used for a land owner of lesser standing that a "Seigneur."

Even PLACE NAMES have changed. In Mississippi, Boardtown became Starkville, Possum Town became Columbus and Webster County became Sumner County. Similar changes took place all across America. Sometimes part of one county was incorporated into another county or one county split to make two.

But, putting it in perspective, once you have the names straightened out, do not be surprised to find the proverbial horse thief hanging from your family tree. I have a pirate hanging from mine. Even fire bug Nero and gangster Al Capone are someone's ancestors.

From distant climes,
o'er widespread seas
we come...
                -George
                Barrington

Immigration

The Huddled Masses

Travel documents were needed by even those who were denied passage. For instance, on May 11, 1637,
> "John Yonge of St. Margarets, Suff. (35) minister & wife Joan (34) & 6 children - John, Tho, Anne, Rachell, Marey, Josueph"

requested to go to Salem, but were forbidden passage from Yarmouth. Even though the family was eventually allowed to go, by the time they were given permission, Joan had died.

Amongst the earliest settlers of the United States were a group of INDENTURED servants who made an agreement of service in exchange for transportation. After working for a sponsor for a specified period of time, the indentured servant was allowed to make a life of their own in the New World. There were documents for them.

Between 1607 and 1825, the largest percentage of immigrants came from Great Britain, Germany, and Africans. But unlike the British indentured servants, the AFRICANS did not immigrate by choice and records for them were not considered necessary.

Research of individual members of specific immigrant groups can be conducted through organizations such as The FINNISH American Heritage Center in Hancock, Michigan. Biographies of Norweigian immigrants can be found in Nordfjordingerhes Historie i Amerika by Lars Gimmestad. And Who's Who Among Pastors in all the Norweigian Lutheran Synods of America, 1843-1927 contains over 2500 biographies.

Names of many of these early white settlers, both indentured and free, can be found in books like *Dictionary of Scottish Emigrants to Canada Before Confederation*, *Fathers of New England*, *Planters of the Commonwealth* and *The Origins of Some Anglo-Norman Families*.

ASIANS, the first coming from CHINA, began arriving in the late 1840's. Their alien registrations and those of others can be found in the National Archives in Washington D.C. was designated as repository for most of these records.

In the mid-1900's, New York, Boston, Baltimore, New Orleans, Philadelphia and Galveston were the busiest ports of entry. Customs lists usually gave the name, age, sex, occupation, date and country of embarkation, date and port of entry and vessel's name for each passenger.

If those alien ancestors decided to become citizens, a number of naturalization documents can typically be found in the National Archives. Among the papers which might be available for any individual alien are -

    1. Declaration of intention
    2. Petition for naturalization
    3. Certificate of naturalization
    4. Oath of allegiance

Any one of those documents could be helpful. For instance, the Certificate of Naturalization should include the person's name, address, birth date, country of origin, physical description, and marital status. If the petitioner was married, the name and vital statistics of the spouse and any children would also be included.

But our ancestors had to go through a lot to get here. Many of the IRISH had to make their way to Liverpool before boarding a ship for America. A steamer could carry 800 adults (2 children counted as 1 adult), who stayed on deck the entire voyage from Ireland to England. Little shelter was provided from storms and no provisions were given to the passengers. They were infirmed and blanketed with each other's vomit.

On board Irish ships to America, the diet consisted of a hardened mixture of wheat, barley, rye, and pease. The emigrant who did the best aboard ship was the one who took biscuits, meat, sugar and coffee or tea along.

Conditions were not good. *Going to America* described a vessel which arrived in Canada in 1846 with 259 passengers. Another seventeen passengers had died on route. The passengers had been given no food and less than a quart of bad water a day during the 41 day crossing. The ship had only 36 berths.

In 1847, the U.S. government began to make laws, changing conditions aboard American-owned ships. The BRITISH had begun passing laws in 1842, but the American laws, called the Passenger Acts, went much further in regulating conditions. The laws were updated and improved almost yearly through 1855. But changes came slowly.

In 1848, the "Ocean Monarch" a three-year-old ship, burned and sank just off Liverpool. Seventy-six died. The "Annie Jane" lost 287 of 351 passengers near the Hebrides.

A study of ships arriving in New York Harbor in 1849 revealed that BELGIUM had the best record of illnesses aboard their ships with no illnesses at all. However, SCANDINAVIAN ships had the worst record of passengers becoming ill. NORWEGIANS began migrating to the United States on the "Restauration" in 1825 from Stavanger to New York City.

Surprisingly, the Scandinavian ships had fewer of their emigrant passengers die, while the FRENCH and Americans had the most. It was not abnormal to have over one hundred of cases of dysentery on a single ship.

Herman Melville described an immigrant ship he sailed on in 1849. When the first storm hit, the moaning and crying from below deck was loud and even the strongest were defeated by seasickness. Melville described them as "stowed way like bales of cotton, and packed like slaves in a slave ship..."

Privacy was a luxury most could not find aboard an emigrant ship. A ticket guaranteed an emigrant with one-fourth of a berth. Most of the time, men and women were assigned berthings together arbitrarily. There was only one toilet per hundred passengers.

In comparison, Nathaniel Hawthorne described a ship he sailed on in 1855. He wrote that "There is no such finery on land, as in the cabin of one of these ships in the Liverpool trade, finished off with a complete panelling of rosewood, mahogany and bird's eye maple, polished and varnished, and gilded along the cornices and the edges of the panels. It is all a piece of elaborate cabinet-work; and one does not altogether see why it should be given to the gales, and the salt-sea atmosphere, to be tossed upon the waves, and occupied by a rude shipmaster, in his dreadnought clothes, when the finest lady in the land has no such boudoir."

In the mid to late 1800's, American ships were larger, with higher decks, and, in general, finer then their British counterparts. However, even passengers on the finest American ship - new, sturdy, clean, and with a doctor on staff - could find a crew who beat and kicked passengers, could have to contend with water or food rationing, and could become seasick.

The U.S. government soon became alarmed at the growing numbers of GERMAN paupers who were able to emigrate to America because of the low rates of passage. Steerage passengers could receive provisions and passage for $16 per adult. The German government declared there was no concerted effort to send Germany's paupers to the New World. They claimed that the poor were only trying to get to the country where men could earn the fantastic sum of $2 a day. But in order to get the $16 needed for the trip, the emigrant had to sell all his clothes and belongings. So when they landed in the United States, they were penniless, unemployed and, in many cases, unable to work.

Despite what the German government said, letters from the overseers of the hospital and the poor house of Grosszimmern, Germany, show that the parish defrayed the cost of passage for "numerous paupers". They claimed that letters from Germans in the United States filled the paupers with stories of jobs, good pay and a better life and that the paupers wanted to go. Grosszimmern paid for 674 paupers and another 100 paid their own passage.
"For each person over twelve year old, 71 florins were paid for passage and board...Each family that was large received a bill of exchange of from 15 to 25 florins, drawn upon the house of Speyer, in New York."
It cost the parish 50,000 florins. In return, "it is true that the titles of the emigrants to the undivided lands in the parishes were made over."

In 1870, Andreas Geyer, Jr. wrote a letter to the German Society of Philadelphia complaining about conditions he witnessed aboard the immigrant ship "General Wayne" skippered by Captain John Conklin. Conklin had promised that they would be given a certain amount of meat, bread, peas, fish, vinegar, butter, potatoes, tobacco, ale and more. During a stop in Portsmouth, England, a British recruiting officer conscripted a number of the men. Geyer wrote,
"But never did I see such a set of miserable beings in my life...After fourteen days had elapsed the captain informed them that they would get nothing to eat except bread and meat. After this each person received two biscuits, one pint of water, and the eighth part of a pound of meat per day. This regulation continued for two

27

or three weeks, when they one and all declared they could not any longer exist on the small allowance they received: that they must, without doubt, perish. The hunger and thirst being at this time so great, and the children continually crying out for bread and drink some of the men, resolved, at all event to procure bread, broke open the apartment wherein it was kept...and actually did, receive after being first tied, a number of lashes on their bare backs well laid on. The whole of the passengers were also punished for this offence. The men received no bread, the women but one biscuit. This continued for nine days, when the men were again allowed one biscuit per day...Five and twenty men, women and children actually perished for the want of the common necessities of life."

Things had not changed very much when the ITALIANS began entering the country in any numbers in the 1880's or when the CUBANS, HAITIANS, and VIETNAMESE emigrated across other large bodies of water to the United States in the late 20th century. In *New Kids on the Block*, a Vietnamese teen described the voyage he took from his land to freedom.

"There were fifty-two people in a twelve-foot-long boat. We could not move. I sat with my knees in my face. I could not lie down... There were military police boats out in the sea looking for the escape boats... We were going to Indonesia. My father knew we shouldn't go to Thailand, because there were a lot of pirates. Most of the people who went to Thailand got killed. After four days we saw a blinking light!... They know the boat people often have money and gold. They steal the females and rape them and force them into prostitution in Thailand. They are pirates... Everybody gave them everything they had, all their savings for their new lives... Every time we saw a big ship we got so happy... Some of the ships said, 'Yes, we take you,' and then when we came close, they tried to hit us to make us drown and die in the sea...if we died, nobody know. So many people were coming out of Vietnam. Other countries didn't want to take any more... In two weeks we saw a ship from Germany with a red cross on it... The Germans took us on board their ship."

And bold and hard
adventures
t'undertake,
Leaving his country
for his country's
sake.
                    -Charles
                    Fitzgeffrey
                    *Sir Francis
                    Drake*

8

Emigration

Yearning to Breathe Free

The first migration to the New World is lost in
prehistory. By 13,000 BC, small groups of men and women had
made the perilous crossing of the Bering Strait; eventually
spreading down the Pacific Coast and extending across the
continent. By the time Columbus arrived in the 15th century,
20 million people, speaking 900 different languages, lived in
what is now North and South America.

A number of countries have come to recognize their loss
of people to emigration and have set aside important papers
documenting that loss. In Hamburg, Germany is the Historisches
auswanderer-Buro (Historic Emigration Office). There is also
Merseyside Maritime Museum in Liverpool, England; Central
Bureau voor Genealogie in The Netherlands; and Utvandrarnas
Hus (The House of Emigrants) in Vaxjo, Sweden.

In addition to uncovering the date ancestors arrived in
the New World from their homeland, many researchers find it
interesting to discover on board what ship they sailed. Many
of those early Americans can be found listed in *The Passenger
and Immigrant Lists Index*, a multi-volumed listing of
immigrants' and *New World Immigrants*, a two-volume
consolidation of passenger lists. Calder's *Passengers on the
"Hector", 1637-1638*, Bank's *The Winthrop Fleet of 1630*, and
Kuhns' *The "Mary and John"; A Story of the Founding of
Dorchester, Massachusetts 1630* are all widely used by
researchers. Other researchers with a hint of a ship's name

or landing date have found the information they need in ship records in the National Archives in Washington, D.C.

To discover why your ancestors left, sometimes it is necessary to do some studying about the conditions of the home country just before they left. Was there a famine? Was there persecution of a specific religion? Also of interest is the discovery of why ancestors left their homeland. Many emigrants were people who became unwilling to accept the either church or state DOCTRINES without question.

According to *Planters of the Commonwealth*, the voyage to the New World cost an adult pilgrim ten pounds and each had to furnish "their own subsistence." Prices were fixed by the Massachusetts Bay Company and adopted by subsequent ships. For families, costs were
> "sucking children not to bee reckoned: such as under 4 yeares of age, 3 for one (fare); under 8, 2 for one; under 12, 3 for 2."

The cost of shipping household items were an additional "4li. a tonn for goods." Since the average voyage was 5-12 weeks long depending upon the weather, winds, and time of year; a good amount of freight was needed simply for subsistence during the trip. An average family with one ton of freight had to pay a great deal for passage on a damp, cold, overcrowded ship. The Massachusetts Bay Co. required immigrants to take along adequate supplies of food, leather, building materials, guns and ammunition, farming implements, household utensils and farm animals.

Miller wrote in *This New Man, the American*, that "poor Puritans were warned that they could not make it on piety alone." In fact so many of the poor were eliminated from the chance to emigrate strictly because of the cost involved.

In *Fathers of New England*, Andrews cited lack of land and poor social conditions along with a restlessness and discontent in England as the chief factors for those who emigrated in the early 1600's. The frustration of living on someone else's land and working that land for someone else's benefit was too much for some. They wanted land of their own. And while RELIGION has been thought to be the major factor of the mass emigration to the New World, Andrews claimed less then one-fifth of those in Massachusetts in the early 1600's were Christians.

But in *This New Man, the American*, Miller argued that if ECONOMICS had been such an important consideration, the Puritans "would not have trusted themselves to the hazards of the sea and the even greater perils of the wilderness." While

they knew God would see them through the hardships they knew
awaited them, they would not expect God to give his blessing
to "a mere real-estate venture."

As time went on, the vast percentage of immigrants
changed to what would be called "blue-collared workers" today.
Few professionals arrived in the 1800's. In 1855, those
immigrants who stated their profession made up the following
percentages.

Profession	Immigrants
Merchants	13.00%
Farmers	30.60%
Laborers	37.50%
Mechanics	13.20%
Teachers	.03%
Clergy	.13%
Lawyer	.19%
Physician	.22%

After early German immigrants appeared to do very well
when they went to the New World, others left behind in Germany
began to dream of making it big in America too. So many German
paupers inundated the country, the U.S. Federal government
unsuccessfully attempted to stop the flow.

Although many Germans emigrated because of deprivation,
there was also a hope for political and religious freedom. The
country of Germany did not exist until the late 1800's. Before
that the Holy Roman Empire, a alliance of hundreds of
principalities, ruled the area until 1806 when it was
dissolved and the Confederation of the Rhine was formed. In
1815, after the Napoleonic Wars, the German Confederation came
into being. Off and on, areas were dominated by France.
Throughout all those changes, the area was never really a
single nation. With each change, political and religious views
of the government also changed. There was no STABILITY.

By 1820, steam vessels had begun to cross the Atlantic.
But in the 1800's, even the best trip involved adversity. Ship
captains dealing in the SLAVE TRADE had more reason to keep
their "passengers" healthy then the captains of emigrant
vessels. Like aboard slave ships, crews frequently beat
passengers.

Emigration from the British Isles was at its heaviest
during the late 1840's and early 1850's, with nearly 2 1/2
million people going to America. In fact, of those emigrating

The Emigrants' Penny Magazine listed three grounds for emigrating in 1850. The reasons given were to REDUCE POPULATION at home, enrich the human condition, and to settle "those vast tracts...lying waste and desolate..." But what it finally boiled down to was that people emigrated for HOPE. As Benjamin Franklin said

> "The only encouragements we hold out to strangers are - a good climate, fertile soil, wholesome air and water, plenty of provisions, good pay for labour, kind neighbours, good laws, a free government,and a hearty welcome."

> Museum: a sort of
> mournful place where
> you conclude that
> nothing could ever
> have been young.
>
> -Walter Pater

9

Sweet Treasures of the Small Town Museum

New Madrid, Missouri has a museum primarily dedicated to its infamous earthquake fault line. The museum at Neenah-Menasha, Wisconsin has 1,800 glass paperweights in its collection. Meridian, Mississippi has dedicated its museum to a favorite son, country singer Jimmie Rodgers. Ardmore, Oklahoma has the Eliza Cruce Hall Doll Museum. Starkville, Mississippi; Princeton, Illinois; and Big Spring, Texas have ones dedicated to the history of their counties.

The American Association of Museums defines a museum as "an organized and permanent non-profit institution, essentially educational or aesthetic in purpose, with professional staff, which owns and utilizes tangible objects, cares for them, and exhibits them to the public on some regular schedule." But that definition is the goal, it must be more loosely applied when considering museums of a small town.

Far more Americans have rural roots than urban ones. Boston, at its inception, was a small town. Some small town museums are called historical societies, and some are called archives; while still others are called museums. Sometimes they are historical parks, forts, or even restored historical homes.

But whether its the Smithsonian or a small town's railroad-depot-turned-museum, a lot more genealogical information can be found in them then most genealogists realize. Of course the Smithsonian has Mary Surrat's gallows hood and leg shackles and Eli Whitney's Cotton Gin, but a small town museum might have Great-Grandma's wedding dress or a picture of Grandma as a young girl. Remember, for every historic figure appearing in the Smithsonian, there are thousands of ordinary people chronicled in small town museums.

But while small town museums are good sources, they are also the most difficult in which to find anything. Granted, a larger percentage of a small community's population will donate to a local museum than a heavier populated area. However, the smaller the town and museum, the higher the probability of the museum being totally staffed by volunteers who have none of the technical knowledge usually needed to competently run a museum. However, those same VOLUNTEERS probably care a lot more about the history of the region and probably know most of the townspeople, living and dead.

Another drawback of a smaller museum is that it usually has more LIMITED HOURS of being open. So as a researcher, check the hours the museum is open before making a trip only to discover the museum closed that day.

But while the quality of the staff of small museums varies and hours can be difficult, the same thing can be said about urban museums. Staff members usually keep 8 to 5 hours, Monday through Friday. So the researcher also needs to check with larger museums to make sure the specific person he needs to talk to is not off-duty.

As a researcher, you might be lucky enough to find that good RECORDS have been kept. And with any luck, those records would contain names of all persons connected with each piece, from those originally owning it to those finally donating it to the museum. But the smaller the museum, the less likely it is that those kind of records will have been kept.

In smaller museums, exhibit cases are often overcrowded with neglected, poorly labeled objects. Therefore, you may have to become a sort of treasure hunter, discovering material without any help. And you can not assume that everything displayed is everything owned. In most cases, museums keep as much of their collection in storage as they keep on display.

Although farm equipment and household items are what most people expect to see in an historical museum, other useful items are there. From STORE LEDGERS you can find out that Great-great Grandpa W.A. Jordan spent $171.40 at Stern and Goodman's Store in 1889 or that Great Grandpa J.B. Perkins purchased table salt for 65 cents and "bluing" for 10 cents in May, 1894.

If the museums is a repository of old PUBLIC RECORDS, you may discover information that in 1904 Great Grandma Lula

Thomas was paid $17.00 a month to teach at Shoot Bag Schoolhouse or that in 1917 Grandpa Lou applied for a passport. You might find J.P. Randle's 1904 subcontract for the Sessumsville/Oktoc postal run for which he was paid $115 a year for a five-hour round trip made six days per week.

Many historical societies and museums have their own libraries of pamphlets, books, newspapers, tapes, histories, manuscripts, and public and private archival-type documents in addition to their general collections.

ORAL HISTORIES have been passed down from person to person for generations. However, it was only recently in the scheme of things, that those oral histories have been written down or otherwise recorded.

Many museums and historical societies have recorded older resident's first person accounts of the past events of their lives or historical events of the town. Most of these early accounts were written. But as technology improved, organizations switched first to tape recorders and home movies and then to video tapes. These oral history collections have become vital links between the people who lived and made the area's history, and the family historian searching for his roots.

Home movies also have been saved and, in many cases, these VISUAL HISTORIES have been transferred to video tape. How wonderful to be able to look into the faces of ancestors years after their deaths!

Family albums are tremendous sources of information which many museums store. Pictures, even tintypes, of ancestors have hopefully been carefully preserved, identified, and filed alphabetically by surname.

Genealogy information can be hiding in almost any place in a museum. Just a few places that might be concealing information about your family include -

Account books	DAR and other club
Bible class pictures	yearbooks
Birth announcements	Diaries
Books	Diplomas
Cemetery records	Doctor's records
Class reunion books	Family albums
Club minutes	Family Bibles
Confederate Veteran	Genealogies
pictures	Grade school pictures
County maps	Letters
County records	Mementos

Newspaper clippings
Newspapers
Old trunks
Photo albums
Pictures of homes and
businesses
Pictures of persons
Recital programs
Reference library
Report cards

Rosters of soldiers of
various wars
Scrapbooks
Servicemen's albums
Store ledgers
Survey records
Teachers' contracts
Wedding invitations
and dresses

Occasionally museums and historical societies send out newsletters or have publications of scholarly or specific nature which they sell. If they have a mailing list, you might want to get on it.

While some visitors take museums like an interstate, speeding through artifacts at high speed, others like to drive back roads at a more leisurely pace. Genealogists generally fit into this latter category. And the purpose of historical museums is to affect the public's perception of history and, in the long run, provide the family historian with unexpected treasures. And small museums offer the sweetest of enticements.

My father invented a
cure for which there
was no disease and
unfortunately my
mother caught it and
died of it.
-Victor Borge
In Concert

10

Causes of Death and Cures That Could Kill

The cause of death of an ancestor is of concern to many
genealogy researchers and of interest to others. In addition
to the genealogy angle, more and more researchers are looking
for medical information in order to uncover genetic tendencies
towards afflictions.

A researcher might find the DISEASE an ancestor in an
obituary, the death certificate, or a mortality schedule.
Mortality schedules for the census years of 1850 through 1880
are listings of persons who died during the year preceding the
census. They included the deceased person's place of birth,
and their month and cause of death.

Sometimes the cause of death can even found on the
tombstone. A stone in St. Michael's Cemetery in Charleston
recounted that in 1819, Robert Buckley died of Yellow Fever at
age 24 years. The Larrabee family monument in Columbus,
Mississippi, listed the cause of death of several members of
the Larrabee family including Frank Larrabee who was "Killed
in Noxubee Co." at age 16.

As with Frank Larrabee, deaths were sometimes UNNATURAL.
One mortality schedule listed such causes of death as
"stabbed", "murdered", "strangled", "scare", "drowned", and
"fall". According to his Smyrna, Tennessee, tombstone
In Memory of Samuel Davis,
a member of the First Tennessee Regiment Volunteers
born October 6, 1842;
died November 27, 1863;
age 21 years 1 month 21 days
"He laid down his life for his country,

37

a truer soldier, a purer patriot,
a braver man never lived
who suffered death on the gibbet
rather than betray his friend and his country."

But even when the cause of death was given, the researcher did not always understand what it was. Michael Carrol of Charleston, South Carolina "died of the illness prevalent among strangers," according to his gravestone. And Andrew Kull reported another tombstone which read "We know he died because he sinned."

Annual reports of area health officers gave clear accounts of diseases in the community. For instance, Dr. W.N. Ames, former chief health officer for Oktibbeha County, Mississippi, wrote in his mylti-paged 1891 annual report that there had been a "prevalence of measles in Sturgis and vicinity" with the "usual appearances of malarial affections (sic)." Had your ancestor died in Sturgis in 1891, he might have died from meales or malaria.

Sometimes the disease listed as cause of death has since been eradicated. Sometimes the name which was frequently used for the disease at the time of death, changed to a completely different name later. For instance, on his tombstone, it was recorded that Benjamin Butler of Norwich, Connecticut, died of "Phthisis Pulmonaris (consumption) in 1787. Sometimes the disease was not common enough for the average person to know much about it. And sometimes early settlers gave their own name for a collection of symptoms.

Some more commonly found, but less clearly understood diseases that a researcher might find would include -

air swellings - air or gas in the intestines.

anchyloses - stiff joints.

ague - a catchall term for symptoms which could have been a cold, influenza, or, sometimes even malaria. The patient suffered from fever, chills, aches, a cough, and, sometimes, a nosebleed.

apoplexy - to be crippled by a stroke. The term was also sometimes used for hysteria or epilepsy.

bilious - suffering from disorder of the liver function, in particular, excess bile secretion. Settlers believed that excess bile brought on headaches, upset stomachs, vomiting, and diarrhea.

bilious fever - excess bile accompanied by high fever and vomiting. Sometimes jaundice was a part of the picture. Symptoms usually included headaches, furred tongue, and pain in the joints. Quinine was considered the medicine of choice.

brain fever - see "meningitis".

Bright's Disease - glomerulonephritis; used as a general term for kidney disease.

bronchitis - serious inflammation of the bronchial tubes and upper portion of the lungs.

camp fever - usually scarlett fever, malaria or thyphus.

catarrh - a general term for any illness involving a sore throat, cough, difficult breathing, and laryngitis.

cerebritus - inflammation of the brain. At the time, it was thought to be caused by long "exposure to a vertical sun," the inordinate use of "ardent spirits", cold fright or injury. Symptoms included fever; flushed dry skin; delirium, blindness and deafness. The application of leeches to a shaved skull was one remedy.

childbed fever - see "puerperal fever".

chilblains - inflammation of the skin occurring in women and children.

cholera - could refer to any of several diseases marked by vomiting and severe gastrointestinal disturbance. In reality, cholera was an acute infectious bacterial disease eventually leading to collapse and frequently caused by drinking contaminated water. It thrived in filth and poverty; and spread rapidly. The disease first appeared in America in 1832. A second invasion attacked from 1849 until 1854.

cholera infantum - disease of vomiting, diarrhea, fever, prostration, and collapse among infants. It mostly occurred during in cities during the summer and frequently was fatal.

cholera morbus - severe gastroenteritis characterized by gripping diarrhea, colic, vomiting. Death could come quickly. Opium and laudanum were used.

chronic - a catchall term for any disease of slow progress, long duration, or frequent recurrence.

clap - gonorrhea.

colic - acute abdominal pains resulting from spasms of a hollow organ and generally attended by distension of the abdomen, primarily in infants. One medication was a solution made up of chloroform, camphor, tannic acid, and morphia.

congestion of the brain - sunstroke.

congested brain - encephalemia; often associated with brain swelling.

consumption - a progressive wasting away of body tissue by tuberculosis. It was thought to be inherited at one time.

croup - inflammation of the larynx, especially in infants, with noticeable periods of difficult breathing, hoarse cough, and laryngitis.

crusted tetter - impetigo.

debility - loss of strength; feeble; weak; infirmed.

diphtheria - communicable disease of nose and throat; with fever, furred tongue and pain. Frequently diphtheria caused the enlargement of heart muscles

dropsy - edema; excessive buildup of clear fluid in body tissues or cavities. Dropsy frequently included edema of the heart area. Generally both sleeping and breathing were difficult.

dysentery - intestinal inflammation, abdominal pain, and passage of mucous and bloody stools. Dysentery might have been caused by bacteria, protozoa, or parasites passed through contaminated food or water. The first known outbreak in America occurred in 1607 in Virginia. Outbreaks continued, especially during wartime. Belladonna was a favorite "cure", as was a mixture of opium, nitric acid and camphor water.

dyspepsia - indigestion; impairment to digestion caused by ulcer, gall bladder disease or inflamed colon.

erysipelas - severe streptococcal inflammation of the skin; accompanied by sore limbs, sore throat and tenderness of glands. Bruised cranberries were sometimes applied to the inflamed area.

febrile - feverish. This could refer to any disease with a high temperature.

flux - excessive, abnormal discharge from the bowels resulting in dehydration.

gastric fever - probably referred to "typhoid".

goiters - a visible enlargement of the thyroid gland. It was not until 1898 that a surgical technique was perfected for goiters.

gout - an overabundance of uric acid in the blood provoking arthritis-like symptoms.

gravel - deposit of small calculous concretions (stones) in the kidneys and bladder.

grippe - acute febrile contagious viral disease identical with or resembling influenza and sometimes causing death.

hydrocephali - also "hydrocephalus" - an abnormal increase of fluid in the cranial cavity. It appears as an enlarged skull, especially the forehead; and deterioration of the brain.

infantile paralysis - polio.

infantile scurvy - also known as "Barlow's disease" - acute scurvy brought about by malnutrition during infancy.

intemperance - excessive drinking of intoxicating liquor. Actually this could have been anything liquor-related, from cirrhosis of the liver to alcohol poisoning to an accident occurring under the influence of alcohol.

intermittent fever - see "malaria".

jaundice - a disease with a yellowing of the skin, body fluids, and tissue due to deposit of bile pigments.

jail fever - see "typhus".

leprosy - a chronic disease causing nodules, loss of sensation, deformities, and eventual paralysis. In the United States, it first appeared along the Gulf Coast, possibly brought to America by slaves.

lingering - dying slowly. This could refer to any chronic disease.

lockjaw - an early symptom of "tetanus". A spasm of the jaw muscles cause the jaw to "lock".

mad dog disease - see "rabies".

malaria - an "ague" occurring periodically - with seemingly frequent relapses. It was a parasitic disease of red blood cells brought on by infected mosquitos. Physicians frequently could not distinguish between malaria and other diseases of the day which produced high fevers. It was thought that malaria was caused by dampness of swamps. Mosquitoes were just thought to be a nuisance.

marasmus - a progressive emaciation caused by malnutrition. Marasmus was more prevalent in very young children suffering from caloric and protein deficiency.

meningitis - inflammation of membranes of the brain or spinal chord.

milk pox - see "white pox".

nightsweats - excessive sweating at night, occurring in pulmonary tuberculosis and other debilitating infirmities.

palsy - full or partial paralysis, or uncontrollable tremor of a portion of the body.

pertussis - severe infectious disease with bouts of spasmodic coughing until the breath is exhausted and ending with a laryngeal (whoop) cough. Pertussis was especially dangerous to infants.

phthisis pulmonaris - see "consumption"

pleurisy - an inflamed pleura (membrane lining of the thorax between the lungs and abdomen) characterized by fever, painful and difficult breathing, and a short dry cough.

pneumonia - a disease including a cough, pains in the side and chest, and difficult breathing. Pneumonia was a particular problem of winter. Ergot mixed with digitalis was a favorite treatment.

poliomyelitis - an acute infectious viral disease which attacked the spinal cord and brain. It was characterized by a high fever, paralysis, and atrophy of the muscles.

puerperal - childbirth

puerperal fever - infection of the placental site following delivery. In serious cases the infection could spread through the uterine wall and/or pass into the bloodstream. It was treated with intra-uterine injections of a carbolic acid solution. Quinine was also used. Morphine eased the pain. The abdomen was painted with tincture of iodine and covered with a warm poultice.

putrid fever - see "typhus."

quinsy - inflamed throat with fever and swelling.

rabies - a viral disease which attacked the brain and spinal cord.

rickets - an insufficient assimilation of calcium and phosphorus caused by inadequate vitamin D and sunlight. Rickets caused deformities when the condition struck during skeletal development.

St. Vistus' Dance - a type of chorea, a disease of the nervous system causing rapid, jerky, involuntary muscle contractions.

scarlatina - see "scarlet fever".

scarlet fever - a severe communicable potent streptococcal disease characterized by skin rash, fever, tonsillitis and generalized toxemia. It frequently caused pulmonary, mastoid and brain abscesses and was most likely crippling or fatal.

scrofula - tuberculosis of the lymph nodes, especially in the neck.

scurvy - swollen knees, shrunken muscles, weakness, depressed spirits, spoiled teeth. An early cure was an extract made from needles and bark of the spruce or balsam tree which provided ascorbic acid. Also used was watercress, "scurvy grass", fresh fruits and vegetables, and lemon and lime juice.

ship fever - see "typhus".

smallpox - severe, eruptive, contagious viral diseases characterized by chills, high fever, back and head aches, and rash. Eruptions from smallpox caused scaring which remained after recovery. An early pamphlet on its treatment called for isolation of every case. "A pest-house remote from habitations should be provided ... but if the patients be kept in a private house it is better that the uppermost rooms of the house be used for the purpose."

spasms - involuntary muscular contraction. The name "spasm" might have been given to any form of convulsions.

summer fever - see "cholera morbus".

summer diarrhea - see "summer complaint".

summer complaint - diarrhea caused by contaminated food. It was found especially in children and was most prevalent in hot weather.

swamp fever - see "camp fever."

sweating sickness - an epidemic-type disease characterized by profuse sweating, high temperature, and early high mortality.

tetanus - an acute infectious disease characterized by spasms in voluntary muscles. The disease is caused by bacteria passed into the bloodstream through a cut

thrush - a fungal disease with white patches on mucous membranes of the mouth.

tremors - trembling or shaking from a physical weakness. This could have referred to any of a number of diseases.

tuberculosis - a communicable disease caused by infection with tubercle bacillus characterized by toxicity of the lungs. Indians were particularly hard hit with about 30% of all Indian deaths between 1911 and 1920 being due to tuberculosis. During the same period, over 35% of all Indians had the disease.

typho-malarial fever - described by one physician in 1891 as "malarial poison." The disease having chronic chills, soreness, toxemia and occasional hemorrhages of the bowels which continued over a long period with a wasting away from high fever. If differed from typhoid in its absence of diarrhea and irregularity of fever. Quinine did not help except to control the temperature. There was soreness or pressure in the anal region and rose-colored spots.

typhoid fever - an infectious bacterial disease characterized by fever, headache, diarrhea and prostration. Temperatures sometimes rose to as high as 106-107 degrees.

typhus - a severe disease remarkable with its high fever, delirium, stupor, intense headaches, deep red rash. It was transmitted to man by lice.

uremia - presence of toxic substances in the blood brought about by inability of the kidneys to filter. Can lead to death.

variola - see "smallpox".

white death - tuberculosis of the lungs.

white plague - see "white death".

white pox - a mild form of smallpox caused by a less virulent strain of the virus.

whooping cough - see "pertussis".

winter fever - see "cholera morbus".

winter itch - an itchiness brought on by extended exposure to cold dry air.

worms - parasites. Hookworms originated in Africa, but were brought to America with slaves. A combination of wormwood tea, oatmeal and male ferns was part of the treatment for tapeworms.

yellow fever - a viral disease of warmer climates transmitted by mosquito. Yellow fever was characterized by fever, prostration, jaundice, and occasional bleeding. Treatment included inducing purging, bleeding to remove poisoned blood, and treating with barks, roots, and herbs. No matter what the treatment, most patients died.

yellow jacket - see "yellow fever."

Sometimes the cause of death left more QUESTIONS then answers, like when all that was listed was the portion of the body involved. Any number of diseases could be described under the listing "bone", "bowels", "digestion" "brain", or "lungs". For instance, "digestion" could have referred to food poisoning, bleeding ulcer, stomach cancer, or any other number of possibilities.

Some of these diseases don't seem especially serious - certainly not something that could kill someone. Other "diseases" that have been listed as cause of death have been "chills, "spasms", "kidney infection", "measles", and "teething". But in those days things were different and simple ailments could become deadly.

During the early days, inoculations were non-existent and diseases became widespread because people didn't know what caused them. People seldom washed their linens or themselves. They believed bathing removed protective oils.

With diseases such as small pox, cholera and yellow fever; fumigation of houses was accomplished with iron pans filled with sulphur, placed in boiling water in a closed room. Cellars, yards, stables, privies and such were treated with a solution of copper as in a barrel of water. Anything coming in direct contact with the ill person was burned. Corpses were washed with a double strength zinc solution, wrapped in a sheet dampened with the zinc solution and buried immediately in as air-tight a coffin as possible.

If those early settlers were lucky, they were treated by a doctor. But many barbers, apothecaries, and blacksmiths practiced medicine too. When there was no professional medicare, people made do.

But even a doctor could be hazardous to a patient's health. During the civil War more soldiers died from disease and treatment than were killed by bullets. Inexperienced doctors dismissed patients before they should have. The sick doctored themselves when they should have been under a doctor's care.

The application for admittance of Elizabeth Miers, age 53 and mother of twelve children, to the Mississippi Lunatic Asylum was signed by two doctors. They listed Mrs. Miers' symptoms as having a loss of memory and incoherent speech, and being sullen and morose. "For the last two weeks she has been suffering from an attack of malarial fever. We think the mania is a mild form due to Uterine disease aggraved lately by a spell of malarial fever." They expected her to "recover entirely." So Mrs. Miers was sent to a lunatic asylum because she was probably suffering from menopause aggravated by malaria.

And sometimes the TREATMENT was more deadly then the disease. Phlebotomy, also known as "bloodletting" or "cupping," was used as a remedy to remove "bad blood" from a patient's body. But it frequently added anemia to the list of ailments. As the patient got weaker and quieter, it was thought he was recoveribng when, in reality, he was dying.

Purging was also considered an antidote for most diseases. One poultice for a wound was made by mashing green persimmons to a pulp. Poultices of bread and milk; and sometimes herbs, oils, or spices; frequently contaminated open wounds. Herbs, potions, and simples were used to cure illnesses while actual cures were ignored.

For teething, leeches were applied behind the ears and gums were lanced. For a sore throat a dirty sock was tied around the patient's neck. And for a bee sting, cow manure was mixed with saliva and applied.

In the late 1800's, one doctor recorded in his personal notebook that "of course opium" was a treatment for diabetes; that "a spray of ether to the epigastric region" would stop "hiccoughs"; and that inhaling "belladonna and strychnine" would cure bronchitis and inhaling mercury would cure diphtheria.

To cure mastitis Dr. Ames suggested putting ice in a beef's bladder and applying it to the inflamed breast. A mixture of rhubarb and soda would supposedly cure nettle rash. And inhaling ether could help Lumbago. To retrieve a foreign object from the ear, dip a pencil in thick glue and hold it in the ear until it sets. Then pull the pencil, and the object stuck to it out of the ear.

A medical book from the same period described how to extract a foreign object from a child's nose by pressing "the vacant nostril so as to close it, and apply you lips close to the child's mouth and blow very hard.

When a fever rose so high that delirium occurred, an olden medical book suggested shaving the patient's head and applying a "blister" to it. The same book suggested applying white paint with a brush to abscesses.

The Vaccination Extension Act of 1853 made it mandatory that all newborn children be vaccinated against smallpox and local registration of those vaccinations were required. Those registrations can be used to verify birth dates. Where birth records are missing, vaccination records can be used as an alternative. Surviving vaccination records can usually be found in local record offices, public health offices or state archives.

So while today people do not die of gout and croup; and while smallpox, polio, and pertussis have almost been eradicated from our country; when our ancestors lived it was quite a different story. And with medical care the way it was, it should have been of no surprise when the patient died.

> Historians have a
> responsibility to make
> some sense of the past
> and not simply to
> chronicle it.
> —Michael Howard
> 1981 review of
> *The Origin of
> History*

11

A Place in Societies

Historical societies, in particular ones on the STATE level, frequently become guardians of indespensible materials. Most state historical societies publish journals and/or newsletters; and sponsor conferences and research; and take part in a number of other preservation endeavors. Many preserve records on microfilm and have computerized family history material, making searches quicker and easier.

For instance, the Historical Society of Michigan has even established The Center for Teaching Michigan History in Ann Arbor. In addition to presenting forums on how to teach history, the center also advises researchers as to what historical resources are available and where they can be found.

On the LOCAL level, genealogical and historical societies meet at regular intervals, presenting programs in interest to their membership. Many have involved themselves in projects, such as publishing cemetery records and other material of historical value, working to preserve historical buildings and even maintaining libraries.

Of particular interest to the genealogist, many historical societies have an official or unofficial genealogist among its membership who will answer queries for little or no charge. The area chamber of commerce usually can put a researcher in contact with the society president.

As with most query letters, a self-addressed stamped envelope and a small check to cover copying costs and, perhaps, a small donation should be included.

INTERNATIONAL historical societies can also provide the genealogist with places to search. Groups like The Federation of Australian Historical Societies in Canberra, Australia and the British Association of Cemeteries in South Asia in London, England can give genealogists leads and addresses. More regional societies, like the Sussex Family History Society in West Sussex, United Kingdom might have the exact information you need.

HERIDITARY societies are organizations you can join because of who your ancestor was or because of something he did. If your ancestor was from Norway or a colonial tavernkeeper or a rider on an orphan train, your ancestry may have been traced already by members of such a society. There are various types of heridesitary societies. Among them are -
1. Military; such as
   Descendants of Mexian War Veterans,
   Daughters of the American Revolution,
   United Daughters of the Confederacy,
   Society of the Whiskey Rebellion of 1794,
   The Society of Cincinati,
   or even The Society of Loyalist Descendants.
2. Professional; such as
   Descendants of Whaling Masters,
   Flagon and Trencher: Descendants of Colonial Tavernkeepers
3. Religion; such as
   Jewish Genealogical Society,
   Friends Historical Society,
   Mennonite Historical Society,
   Alabama Baptist Historical Society.
4. Early Settlers; such as
   National Society of Colonial Dames of America,
   General Society of Mayflower Descendants,
   Native Sons of the Golden West,
   Society of Descendants of Colonial Hispanics,
   Sons of the Republic of Texas,
   The Order of the First Families of Mississippi 1699-1817.
5. Family Names; such as
   Landon Family Research Group,
   Veitch Historical Society,
   Southern Bailey's,
   Austin Families Association of America.
6. National Origin; such as
   Sons of Norway,

Genealogical Society of Flemmish Americans,
The Welsh Society,
Czech Heritage Foundation,
Society for Spanish and Portuguese History,
Alliance of Trasylvania Saxons,
Bavarian National Association of North America,
Sons of Italy in America,
Byelorussian Congress Committee,
Chinese Historical Society of America,
Genealogical Society of Hispanic America,
St. Andrews Society (Scots).
7. Ethnic; such as
American Indian Historical Society,
Afro-American Historical and Genealogical Society,
Creole-American Genealogical Society,
Asia Society.
8. Groups; such as
Orphan Train Heritage Society of America,
Descendants of the Illegitimate Sons and Daughters
of the Kings of Britain,
First Families of the State of Franklin,
International Genealogy Fellowship of Rotarians.
9. Mixture; such as
American Lithuanian Roman Catholic Women,
American Historical Society of Germans in Russia.
As with historical societies, hereditary societies also
conduct forums and workshops, publish newsletters and/or
journals, and answer queries.

Also useful to the family historian is the FRATERNAL
organization, which unites people with specific interests.
Sometimes ethnicity or religion is the uniting factor. Other
times its
Professional; such as
The International Order of Hoo-Hoo (Lumbermen),
Fraternal Order of Police,
Showmen's League of America,
Hawaii Sugar Planters Association.
And sometimes the thing that unifies the group is purely
Social; such as
Loyal Order of Moose,
Grand United Order of Odd Fellows,
Loyal Order of Buffaloes,
Ancient Free and Accepted Masons.

Freemasonry is the largest of all the fraternal groups,
with a Grand Lodge in every state and local lodges in many
communities. It has been around a long time and books, such as
*1819-1849 Abstradex of Annual Returns: Mississippi Free and
Accepted Masons*, provide names of early settlers and locate

them in an area of a state by naming the lodge. Other important material, such as death dates are frequently included.

While both depend upon the ancestor, fraternal organizations differ from hereditary organizations in that descendants will not become members in fraternal ones unless they are inclined to follow in their ancestors footsteps interest-wise. But the information kept about both former and present members in sometimes quite detailed.

              12

          Letting Cemeteries Talk

    Wordsworth was wrong when he wrote "toward the silent
tomb we go." The tomb is far from silent for the genealogist
who knows how to "listen".

    Compared with today's stark granite tablets, older
monuments and stones are more interesting and simply scream
with information. They are usually artistically decorated
with flowers, urns, cherubs, caskets, or even sometimes,
portraits of the deceased.

    In fact, the stone itself can give some clues about the
person. Monument decorations might be chosen to reflect an
occupation, military service, or gender. Prominent and
affluent families frequently have larger monuments and are
frequently found in a family plot in the cemetery. The
dominant couple of the family are usually found in the center
of the family plot with their children, with smaller
tombstone, surrounding them.

    There are a number of types of cemeteries; including
church, public, family, and special use cemeteries. Family
cemeteries are usually found on the old homestead. Special use
cemeteries include confederate and other military ones.
Arlington National Cemetery is a special use cemetery.

    Large monument-filled public cemeteries in large cities
have offices which can provide maps of the cemetery, saving
search time. Their records might include burial permit records
and, even grave opening records. Individual churches maintain
their own burial records, while the best source for a list of
those buried in a small town's cemeteries is the local
historical society or library. Even if they don't know where

an out-of-the-way cemetery is, they usually know who would know.

Older area residents can guide you to family burial places, containing several generations. Southerners often buried their dead on their farms. Pioneers were buried along the trails. Today these graves are often "lost" and finding them can be time consuming.

Once a grave site has been found, care should be taken in deciding which data to accept. As described in an earlier chapter, there are two types of evidence. A primary source of evidence was an eyewitness to an event, was concerned with it and/or recorded it immediately. A mother would know her child's name and birthplace and date.

But a daughter who heard the information years before may not be considered a primary source for information concerning her father's birthplace. She would be a secondary source. Only the date and place of death on the gravestone would be primary information.

A Southold, Long Island stone erected years after his death, claimed that Nathan Landon was born in Wales. In reality, Nathan's father was born in England, probably near the Welsh border. The name on the tombstone might vary depending upon who commissioned the stonecutter. Some descendant of Nathan with mistaken information, erected the monument to Nathan and his wife. Secondary information can be incorrect.

And the name confusion can be exacerbated when more than one person buried in the cemetery has the same name. Christopher Youngs had John and Christopher, who each named sons Christopher, leaving four people in the same small hamlet with the same name at the same time.

Once the names have been straightened out, an amazing amount of information can be found on tombstones. A marker at the Old Presbyterian Cemetery in Starkville, Mississippi, reads,

Arunah Bardwell, M.D.

a native of Mass.

a resident of N.C. for 20 years

and of Oktibbeha county for the last five

d. Oct. 25, 1938 in the 55th year of his age.

From one gravestone we have learned that Arunah was a doctor who was born in Massachusetts where he lived circa 1883 through 1913; that he lived in North Carolina from circa 1913 through 1933; and that he lived in Oktibbeha County, Mississippi from circa 1933 until his death in 1938. Since he lived in Massachusetts from birth until age 30, that is where he probably married and, possibly, had children. Licenses and birth certificates might be found there.

Aside from the BIRTH and DEATH dates, information revealed on tombstones can fall into a number of categories. Dr. Bardwell's tombstone contains something most stones do not. His PROFESSION is listed. He was probably a medical student in Massachusetts sometime between 1901 and 1910. There might be records at his medical school. He also might have been a member of a medical association or on staff at a hospital.

A marker at the Odd Fellows Cemetery in Starkville reads

Our Pastor, 1857-1899
Rev. T.G. Sellars
August 27, 1831
March 11, 1899

While not as much data is given on this stone, it does suggest checking with local churches and asking about church histories.

But some stones tell a great deal about a person's professional life. For instance, the inscription on a stone in Charleston, South Carolina reads

Sacred to the memory of
Rev. Andrew Fowler, A.M.
Who died 29th Decr. 1850;
aged 91 years and 6 months.
He was admitted to Deacons orders in June 1789,
And to Priests orders in June 1790
By the first Bishop of New York.
After several years of pastoral duty in
The Diocese's of New York and New Jersey,
he was Elected Rector of
St. Bartholomews Parish, So. Ca. 3rd Feby. 1807
During the remainder of his life,
he was engaged in the faithful discharge
of the duties of the ministry,
in connection with this Diocese
As parish priest, missionary and author,
he labored earnestly and usefully
in the inculcation of
the principles and precepts
of true Christian piety, as Embodied

54

from the Bible in the system of the Church
which he served and which he
well understood and truly loved.
When age and infirmity
prevented more public exertion,
his conversation and example
continued to illustrate
and enforce the religion
Of that Savour, in who he finally sleeps.

While the arrangement of gravestones provide clues of
RELATIONSHIPS, some relatives, may not be buried near each
other. Brothers will be buried with their wives, not with
their parents or near each other. Family members might be
spread across a cemetery.

In a cemetery in Ansonia, Connecticut a monument informs
visitors that Mrs. Hannah Clark, who died in 1801 at the age
of 91, left 333 direct descendants at the time of her death -
10 children, 62 grandchildren, 242 great-grandchildren, and 19
great-great-grandchildren. So a number of Clarks might be
expected to be found buried in the cemetery.

Names of parents or other relatives frequently appear on
tombstones. In Starkville, Mississippi, we learn from his
tombstone that George D. Deavenport was the son of Dr. M and
M.A. Deavenport of Okalona, Mississippi.

Another stone in Charleston, South Carolina's St.
Michael's Church reported

IN
affectionate remembrance
To
SARAH ANNA
Daughter of Capt. Wm. and Harriet Brown
and wife of
Robert L. Baker
who died at Phildela. Pen.
on the 17th. Septr. 1839
aged 23 yrs, 24 days.

Other epitaphs discuss the CAUSE OF DEATH. According to
the monument for the Larrabee family in the Friendship
Cemetery in Columbus, Mississippi, Frank Larrabee was "Killed
in Noxubee Co." at age 16, Lucy died of "bronchitis" at age
37, Lucy E. died of "Typhoid fever" at age 4, and Edward died
of "convulsions" at age 2.

According to his tombstone, 1st Lt. Lee Watson Johnson fought in the Philippines on Bataan under McArthur in World War II was taken prisoner and in October, 1944 met with "a tragic death in the South China Sea."

John Gidley's son died because of "a violent Explosion of Gun-Powder eleven Days before he expired." And, according to her tombstone, Miranda Bridgeman

> fell prey to the Flames
> That consum'd her father's House
> ...Anxious for those who slept above
> She ventured on the trembling floor
> It fell, she sank, & rose no more.

According to his tombstone in Calvary Baptist Cemetery in Winston County, Mississippi, Charilie Burris, the fifteen year old son of Giles and Sarah Burris, was "shot wile hunting."

But probably most interesting is the odd epitaph of Warren Gibbs of Pelham, Massachusetts, who died "by arsenic poison" in 1860. The poem on his stone goes into more detail.

> Think my friends when this you see
> How my wife hath dealt by me
> She in some oysters did prepare
> Some poison for my lot and share
> When of the same I did partake
> And nature yielded to its fate.
> Before she my wife became
> Mary Felton was her name.
> Erected by his Brother
> Wm Gibbs

In Pepperell, Massachusetts a gravestone tells the visitor that "Neh'h" Hobart's
"death was caused by falling backwards, on a stick, as he was loading wood. Nobody present, but his grandson, who lived with him...his death remarcable!" (sic)

Frequently, MILITARY SERVICE is recorded on a memorial, like these from an Oddfellows Cemetery in Starkville, Mississippi.

Capt. William Hillhouse	Samuel B. Critz	Jas. W. Howard
Neil's	Pvt. 2 State Tr	1842-1912
S.C. MIL	Miss. Inf. C.S.A.	CSA 1861-1865
Rev. War	July 24, 1848	Columbus Rifleman
(no dates)	Sept. 7, 1940	Co., Columbus Miss

Not only do these stones report military service, they give the wars and states . Military records, including war pension papers, usually contain a great deal of family history.

In those cases when the exact age is given at the time of death, the exact date of birth can be determined. But it needs to be remembered that in 1752, an eleven-day calendar change took place.

PERSONALITY TRAITS frequently show up on tombstones. In Old Town Burying Ground in Ansonia, Connecticut, appears the stone for "The widow Sarah Tutle (d. 1769) whose character in Life was that She was a virtuous woman."

Adjacent stones in a cemetery in New Hampshire tell of a married couple -

SACRED	SACRED
to the memory of	to the memory of
AMOS FORTUNE	VIOLATE
who was born free in	by sale the slave of
Africa, a slave in America	Amos Fortune, by Marri-
he purchased liberty	age his wife; by her
professed Christianity,	fidelity his friend and
lived reputably, &	solace, she died his widow
died hopefully	Sept. 13, 1802
Nov. 17, 1801	AEt. 73
AEt. 91	

SPOUSES are usually buried near each other. But in addition, many stones record spouses. Near the entrance in the Old Burying Ground in Fairfield, Connecticut are identical, adjacent gravestones for "Mrs. Abigail Squier, Wife of Samuel Squier Esq." The only difference between the two stones is that one has a 1780 death date at the age of 55, and the other has a 1785 death date at the age of 52. Samuel must have married two Abigail's.

Seven large stones in a cemetery in Haverhill, Massachusetts, for Nathaniel Thurston and six of his wives - Betsey (died 1790 at age 34); Martha (died 1799, age 32); Huldah (died 1801, age 24); Clarrissa (died 1803, age 36); Martha (died 1804, age 25); and Mary (died 1808, age 27). Nathaniel's seventh wife survived him and chose not to be buried with her predecessors.

And then, in Rhode Island appear the curious stones of "Lidia the Wife of Mr. Simeon Palmer" and "Elizabeth who should have been the Wife of Mr. Simeon Palmer."

Starkville, Mississippi has this strangely phrased tombstone.

> Mrs. L. A. Davis
> b. January 3, 1809
> d. June 6, 1868
> Married I. N. Davis
> 2nd time March 12, 1857
> Married S. C. Muldrow
> Nov. 14, 1826
> 1st husband

Some have chosen to use a tombstone to make POLITICAL AND SOCIAL COMMENTS, like the odd inscription on a monument in Milford, Connecticut -

> "Molly tho pleasant in her day
> Was suddenly seiz'd and sent away
> How soon shes ripe how soon shes rott'n
> Sent to her grave, & soon forgott'n."

According to Julia Bales Noe Callaway's tombstone in the Emma Jarnigan Cemetery in Hamblin County, Tennessee, she was "a devoted Christian, Mother, Civic Worker and Leader in Republican politics."

And what begins as a tribute to Joseph Brainerd ends as something completely different. He "was wounded and taken prisoner by the Rebels in the Wilderness; May 5, 1864 was sent to Andersonville Prison Pen in Georgia where he died on the 11th day of Sept. 1864, entirely and wholly neglected by President Lincoln and murdered with impunity by the Rebels, with thousands of our loyal Soldiers by Starvation, Privation, Exposure, and Abuse."

In Danvers, Massachusetts a large monument was erected to Rebecca Nurse. "Accused of Witchcraft She declared, 'I am innocent and God will clear my innocency'. Once acquitted yet falsely condemned She suffered death July 19, 1692."

Monuments in Walpole, New Hampshire were erected by the descendants of the two men who each claimed to be the founder of the city. The granite monument to John Kilburn and the marble monument to Col. Benjamin Bellows each states that the man was the founder of Walpole.

Frequently SOCIAL STANDING of the deceased can be determined by the placement and size of the monument. Many have tried to obtain immortality by building pretentious monuments. In Center Grove, Mississippi, descendants erected a memorial to "Squire Harpole". On Shelter Island, New York is another such shrine indicating social standing.

TO
NATHANIEL SYLVESTER,
FIRST RESIDENT PROPRIETOR
OF
THE MANOR OF SHELTER ISLAND,
UNDER GRANT OF CHARLES II.
A.D. 1666;
[arms]
AN ENGLISHMAN
INTREPID,
LOYAL TO DUTY,
FAITHFUL TO FRIENDSHIP,
THE SOUL OF INTEGRITY AND HONOR,
HOSPITABLE TO WORTH AND CULTURE,
SHELTERING EVER THE PERSECUTED FOR CONSCIENCE' SAKE;
[erected by]
THE DAUGHTERS
OF
MARY AND PHOEBE GARDINER HORSFORD,
DESCENDANTS OF
PATIENCE, DAUGHTER OF NATHANIEL SYLVESTER
AND
WIFE OF THE HUGUENOT BENJAMIN L'HOMMEDIEU
IN
REVERENCE AND AFFECTION
FOR
THE GOOD NAME OF THEIR ANCESTOR
IN 1884
SET UP THESE STONES
1610   FOR A MEMORIAL   1680

And sometimes a stone will give MORE THAN EXPECTED. In the Oddfellows Cemetery is the grave of Martha A. Walker. From it we learn her husband was Abram Walker; she was born November 12, 1816 in Chatham Co., North Carolina; she died in her home in Starkville, Mississippi on November 26, 1880; and she lived to the age of 64 years and 11 days. Sometimes even the hour of death is listed.

Other stones give entire life histories of the deceased, like a stone in St. Michael's Episcopal Cemetery.

In memory of EDWARD JENKINS D.D.
who died in April 1821 in Flamorganshire
in Wales, the place of his nativity. He
was educated at Jesus College Oxford,
And having removed to this Country.

was successively, Rector of the Churches
of St. Bartholomew, St. Michael's, his
orthodox principles as a Minister of the
Gospel, his abilities as a Preacher, his
candor, probity and benevolence,
his exemplary pious, and moral conduct
graced with the acquirements of the Scholar,
And polished manners of the Gentleman,
designated his as well qualified
for the dignified station of
Bishop of South Carolina,
to which he was elected Decr. 20, 1804,
and which he declined, apprehensive
that his advanced age, might impede,
the punctual discharge of its duties.
Bereaved by the death, of the Issue he had
by his beloved wife, a native of the State,
He showed a Parental kindness,
to the children and grandchildren,
whom she had by a former husband,
They to record his worth, and their gratitude,
Here place this inadequate Memorial.

In the same cemetery, the gravestone of Harriet Fowler
even reported that she had been the third daughter of Andrew
and Mary Fowler, she had received communion in the Episcopal
church at age 14, and she had been sick for three years prior
to her death.

A number of symbols that show up on headstones provide
clues for the genealogist. Members of the Masons and the
American Legion might have their organizational emblems on
their stones. Crests or coats-of-arms also appear sometimes.
But regard coats-of-arms with skepticism. A Star of David
would indicate a Jewish background: a cross would indicate a
Christian one.

When visiting cemeteries for genealogy purposes, remember
the Golden Rule and treat the burial sites as you would like
yours treated by your descendants one hundred years from now.
Do take flowers. The people who once lovingly cared for the
graves are probably long gone themselves. And even though
most cemeteries are lovely, grassy areas with large trees, do
not picnic in the cemetery.

If you would like to read more about interesting cemetery
inscriptions, read *New England Cemeteries: A Collector's Guide*
by Andrew Kull.

Benjamin Franklin's 1725 self-composed epitaph seems an appropriate closing for a discussion on tombstones.

"The body of Benjamin Franklin, Printer, (Like the cover of an old books, its contents torn out and script of its lettering and gilding.) Lies here food for worms; But the work shall not be lost, for it will (as he believed) appear once more in a new and more elegant edition, revised and corrected by author."

There was a Birth,
certainly, we had
evidence and no doubt.
                    -T.S. Elliott
                    Journey of the
                    Magi

13

Attacking the Courthouse

When they hear the words "courthouse records" most
genealogists think only of marriage, death and birth records.
But in the early years of our country, those vital statistics
were usually thought to be the domain of the church. And most
states did not record births, deaths and marriage until quite
late in the scheme of things - usually the late 1800's or
early 1900's. But other records were kept during those earlier
times, and an enormous amount can be found using them.

For instance, the plentiful land of the New World was a
tremendous enticement for those first immigrants. And from the
day those first Americans divided up their land, records have
been kept of all LAND transactions. And those transactions
have generally been considered the domain of the county or
parish.

The land records (chancery) or tax collector's office
should have early MAPS of the county with names of landowners
marked. Typically, counties sell county maps with ranges,
townships and sections marked. These can be useful keeping
track of family lands.

Land purchases were frequently made in both the husband's
and wife's name. Upon marriage, a son might have been deeded
a portion of his father's land. After his death, a father's
land was customarily deeded over to his children. Individuals
who witnessed the signing of deeds may have been relatives.

And frequently family members settled on nearby land. For
instance, Aaron and Simeon Balch who owned land in the same
section of land in Lapeer, Michigan were found to be brothers
whose families had gone west together. William Reynolds turned

out to be the son of John Reynolds who lived next door to him in Mcomb County, Michigan.

A 1910 "map and farm directory" for Armada Township, Michigan showed Albert Wilson with 209 acres, Rob Wilson with 40 acres, and Mary Wilson with 107 acres in Section 6; adjoining land in Section 5 which owned by Peter Wilson with 150 acres and Sarah Wilson with 45 acres. And, in nearby Section 4, James Wilson owned 120 acres. These people were probably related.

But before beginning to work with land records, you need to familiarize yourself with the basic terminology, such as "section", "township", "range", "plat", "lien", "grantee" and "grantor" to help you understand.

MILITARY RECORDS are overlooked materials also found in the county courthouse. East of the Mississippi River, there should be records at least as far back as some Civil War. Even in the 1860's, whenever civilians signed up for the Confederate or Union side, they were registered in a county ledger. Information kept in those books varied, depending upon the area, from just the soldier's name to a brief history of the soldier's military career. Then after the war, many counties continued to keep track of their Civil War veterans and their wives or widows.

And the more recent the military service, the more precise and complete the information kept on each soldier signing up for military service in the county. Military discharge records for well into the 1900's also are frequently available.

While wills obviously list family members; other, lesser used PROBATE RECORDS also contain information. Guardianship or transfers of custody of minor children might contain the names of a child's parents and siblings and even other relatives who became the child's guardian. For example, probate records for Lowndes County, Mississippi include those for the children of Calvin McCracken. In addition to the names of all of Calvin's minor children, the records give the death date for Calvin and the name of Calvin's father, John McCracken, who was becoming the children's legal guardian and taking them to Lawrence County, Tennessee.

Payment of administrator or executor bonds, the liquidation of the deceased's debts, inventory of the estate and division of the estate among heirs all are additional probate records a genealogist might find on file.

Dockets for pending legal action might be maintained under various titles, depending upon the locality. Some of the more frequently used names for local courts include criminal, civil, superior, family, circuit, justice, chancery and small claims courts.

Family or civil COURT RECORDS might include guardianship, divorce, probate, adoption and insanity cases. For instance, you might learn that in the 1880's ancestor Mary Jane Askins was admitted to a lunatic asylum because she was suffering from depression. According to the records, at first Mrs. Askins tried to run away, then destroyed her bedclothes and finally refused to get out of bed or speak.

Criminal court records might include a coroner's report, trial transcript, pardons or probation records. Admittedly, coroner reports contained little genealogical information, with the exception of date and time of death. But inquest testimony can provide much more biographical information about the deceased. So while of course the death certificate is the most important; an inquest transcript can be used to verify death certificate information.

But you may not like what you find in criminal records. Crimes can range anywhere from murder to slander to perjury to non-attendance at church. You might discover that in 1875, ancestor William Rogers was convicted of Grand Larceny or that in 1878, ancestor William Johnson was sentenced to seven days in jail for failing to perform road duty. But better to be a descendant of Misters Johnson or Rogers then discovering you are descended from a convicted murderer.

Or you might find your ancestors in both civil and criminal records, like the descendants of Macon and Mary Davis did. In 1875, Macon was arrested for assault and battery on Mary. After hearing the testimony of witnesses, the judge found both plantiff and defendant guilty and fined them $500 each. Their divorce appears in civil court records for 1877.

The Superintendent of EDUCATION's annual lists of eligible children usually contain the names of the parents or guardians, district, and names and ages of all school aged children. While early records lack uniformity, the information in them is invaluable, especially in putting together family units.

Other records in a courthouse that can be of obvious help but are seldom considered include NATURALIZATION PAPERS, PASSPORT APPLICATIONS, VOTER REGISTRATION FILES and, even more importantly, NAME CHANGES.

However, information collection and recording procedures vary from state to state. Sometimes the important records will be in the town hall, sometimes in the courthouse and sometimes in the state archives. And some states did not even mandate the keeping of vital records until well into the twentieth century.

Attacking a courthouse by mail is usually a fruitless effort. If you are sent an answer to your query, unless it is photocopied, consider it a secondary source. In addition to being unfamiliar with older records, county officials do not care the same way you do about your research and do not put in the time you would.

Much of the time, county officials will only go through marriage, birth, and death records for specific years, and then only for a set fee. Many county workers look at genealogy queries as a real pain. In their defense, American counties don't have limitless budgets, and their employees are frequently underpaid, overworked and simply don't have the time to search.

In addition, county workers don't use old records on a regular basis and are unfamiliar with them. Many do not even know what records the county holds as it doesn't come up as part of their daily job. When asked where a particular estate record book was recently, a records clerk replied "Don't use it, don't know about it, and don't care."

Be prepared to find the records you need someplace other than the courthouse. Frequently, older records have been consigned to the courthouse basement, the public library or the local museum. Many record clerks don't even know where the records have been taken. So it is also quite possible for courthouse officials to send you to the public library only to have the librarians send you back to the courthouse because they don't have the records either.

Another problem with courthouse research is knowing which courthouse to go to. Some counties have more than one courthouse. Borders change and a county might absorb a portion of or break off from another county. County names change, sometimes several times. In Louisiana, they are called parishes, not counties.

One piece of land in Mississippi was first in Monroe County, then became part of Lowndes County when it was organized. The land became part of Colfax County when that county was organized from pieces of three other counties. Then, finally, Colfax changed its name to Clay County. Land records from the 1840's for that particular piece of land are found in the Clay County Courthouse. But estate records from the same time period, for the owners of the same piece of land, are found in the Lowndes County Courthouse.

Another problem occurs when people owning land in one county also owned land in a neighboring county. This makes things especially difficult when the neighboring counties are also in bordering states.

And adding to the problem of using unusual county records is that, with the exception of the land records, most prior to 1800, or even later in the west, were never indexed.

That is, if the records were kept properly in the first place. Dr. Ames, chief of health officer for Oktibbeha County, Mississippi described the problem with vital records in his 1891 annual report.

"There is no method known to me where practicing physicians can be induced to make reports of the births and deaths in their practice... Even if such reports were faithfully made by every physician the records would not be complete because numbers of negro children are born yearly unknown and unintended by physicians and the same can be said... with reference to deaths for many die having never received medical treatment especially among the Negros... A law must be constructed with a penalty attached before vital statistics can be made accurate and reliable."

Although courthouses are routinely opened from 8 a.m. to 5 p.m. Monday through Friday, be prepared for exceptions. Courthouse offices in lesser populated areas have been known to close down from noon to 1 p.m. for lunch, with staff herding all visitors out of the building for the hour. Obscure holidays celebrated by few are always celebrated by county employees. And in the South, Robert E. Lee's birthday is still alive and well.

But despite the problems of working with courthouse records, the extra work is worth it. Remember, it is nearly impossible to find the exact location of the old family homestead without a land record or county map.

14

The Broad Use of Broadsides

The broadside preceded the news-sheet, which proceeded
the newspaper as a method of imparting news. It was a sheet of
paper with something such as a ballad, or an announcement, or
an advertisement, printed on it. Many times information given
on an old broadside could prove to be very important to the
genealogist. During the late 1600's through the 1700's,
broadsides were at their most popular. But they became of less
historical interest after 1800, as the newspaper improved as
a mode of communication.

However, even then, the ballad, as presented on the
broadside did continue as a propaganda instrument used by both
the North and the South during the Civil War. Both
Revolutionary and Civil War ballads briefly documented major
incidences, such as the surrender of Fort Sumter, the Battle
of Bull Run, the arrest of Southern sympathizers.. One 1863
eight-line poems listed the faults of General Benjamin Burler,
calling him a brute, coward, beast, ruffian, sot, thief, and
liar, among other things. A number of other broadsides
described Col. Elmer Ellsworth's murder for removing the
Confederate flag from the staff at an Alexandria, Virginia
hotel. James Jackson, manager of the hotel and the man who
shot Ellsworth, was then murdered by Corporal Francis Brownell
from Ellsworth's company. That incident became a propaganda
item for both Northern and Southern sympathizers.

Any broadside containing a person's name is a potential
help for a family historian. Another one from the Civil War
era read
"John Merryman was snatched from his family and lodged in
Fort McHenry, but Beauregard and Davis will punish the
champagne-drinking gluttons who arrested Merryman, robbed
widows, and killed orphans."

From this broadside the genealogist discovers an interesting event, to say the least, in the life of one of his or her ancestors.

Similarly, broadsides from the Revolutionary War era described the 1775

"...Bloody engagement that was Fought on Bunker's Hill In Charlestown New England, On the 17th of June, 1775; Together with some Remarks of the Cruelty and Barbarity of the British Troops, by Destroying the above mention'd Town by Fire..."

And another broadside declared

"We came, we saw, byt could not beat, and so - we sounded a retreat..."

The earliest examples of English broadsides were usually associated with the CHURCH. But then from the 16th century on, the broadside served a number of GOVERNMENTAL purposes, like announcing acts of Parliament and new local laws, and giving notice of executions. Many of these contained the names of persons who held political offices. For instance, a number of Thomas Pownall's proclamations, like his March 12, 1759 call for a public fast, were published during his tenure. The names of Francis Bernard, William Shirley, Thomas Danforth, William Dummer, and many other leaders appeared in broadsides of the 17th and 18th centuries. Such proclamations might begin such as

"By His Excellency, Joseph Dudley, Esq; ... A Proclamation For an Embargo on Ships and Vessels bound to Barbados, and the Creeby Leeward Islands ... Dated October 30, 1705."

From it, a genealogist can learn something about his or her ancestor's position and probable dates the ancestor held the office.

Broadsides also served as an inexpensive, easily circulated weapon for political and personal CONTROVERSIES, like the broadside written by my ancestor Samuel Sewall. It was interesting to discover his view originally in volume 1 page 545-548 of the second edition of The Athenian Oracle, printed at London in 1704.

"Quest. Whether Trading for Negroes i.e. carrying them out of their own Country into perpetual Slavery, be in it self Unlawful, and especially contrary to the great Law of Christianity? Boston of the Massachusetts; December 5, 1705."

As a broadside, Samuel's work was printed by Bartholomew Green, and sold by Samuel Phillips "at the Brick shop above the Town-House".

Listings of the names of persons for or against controversial issues frequently showed up on broadsides following notices of meetings such as the November 3, 1773,
"Tradesmen's Protest against the Proceedings of the Merchants. Relative to the New Importance of Tea."
and
"...List of those Persons who signed an Address to the late Governor Hutchinson, on his Departure for England, with their several Occupations, Shops, Stores or Places of Abode..."

Satires, ballads, almanacs, and even last words of dying criminals all found their way onto broadsides. One such was
"The Declaration and Confessions of Jeffry, Negro, who was executed at Worcester, October 17, 1745, for the Murder of his Mistress, Tabitha Sanford, at Mendon, the 12th of September preceding..."

And FUNERAL VERSES, like the following could excite any genealogy researcher.
"The following Thoughts came from a Youth Scarce 15. The following Lines wrote by a Youth AEt. 16 were designed for the Consolation of the late Rev. Dr. Mayhew's spouse."
The broadside, which was pinned to Mrs. Mayhew's casket, gives a genealogist more information and an incite into the feelings of ancestors seldom seen by a researcher.

And imagine the excitement a Hirst/Sewall researcher might feel upon finding a broadside reading
"In Remembrance of Mr. Samuel Hirst, The Eldest, and only Surviving Son of Grover Hirst, Esq; Merchant, & Elizabeth Sewall his Wife ... was born at Boston, October 23, 1705. And died very suddenly, when he was in his way upon the Long 'Wharff, at two in the Afternoon, January 14, 1726."
And the descendants of John Foster struck gold when they discovered the
"Funeral Elegy Dedicated to the Memory of His Worthy and The Learned & Religious Mr. John foster who Deed in Dorchester the 9 of Sepbr 1681."
A number of family researchers would be pleased to discover the broadside from Salem, Massachusetts, dated June 25, 1773. It read
"Verses on the sudden and awful Death of Mrs. Rebecca Giles, Mr. Paul Kimball and his Wife, Mrs. Desire Holman, Mr. William Ward and his wife, Miss Esther Madury, Mr. Nathaniel Diggadon and his Wife, and Mrs. Sarah Becket, all of Salem who were drowned all together off this Harbour on the 17th Day of June, 1773. Boston: Printed and sold in Milk-Street."

Since colonial readers were interest in all sort of NEWS, including the comings and goings of people and ship, broadsides also provided that information. These Salem broadsides declared

"...Yesterday Captain Hill in the Brig, arriv'd at Marblehead..."

and

"...This Day at Noon, Captain John Derby, in a Schooner arrived here..."

That information could be of great interest to the descendants of Captains Hill or Derby. And sometimes GOSSIP brought home by these travellers from overseas was considered newsworthy and was published. One example was defined time-wise as closely as possible. It read

"Salem: Wednesday, Nov. 1, one o'clock, P.M. We have this moment, received the following great and important intelligence from Capt. Stephen Lowater, who arrived at Ipswich yesterday in 14 days from Liverpool..."

Exiled British printer Thomas Fleet opened a shop in Boston and proved that murders, fires, earthquakes, and executions could make money on the streets of Boston. Broadsides like the 1727

"...Proclamation For Apprehending John Pittman (suspected of murdering Capt. James Cornwall)..."

and

"...Strange and Wonderful Predictions of Mr. Love, minister of the Gospel at Lawrence-Jury, who was beheaded on Tower-Hill in the Time of Cromwell's Government of England..."

later gave exciting tidbits to descendants of Pittman, Cornwall, and Love.

In fact, some of these broadsides appeared to be more like the predecessor of today's tabloids then today's newspapers, as demonstrated below.

"A Dialogue between Elizabeth Smith and John Sennet, who were convicted before his Majesty's Superior Court, Elizabeth Smith For Thievery, and John Sennet for Beastiality! and each sentenced to set upon the Gallows for the space of one Hour, with a Rope round their Necks Elizabeth Smith to receive Twenty Stripes upon her naked Back, and John 'Sennet, Thirty-nine."

However, the descendants of Sennet and, possibly, Smith, might rather not discover that broadside.

Although broadsides have the potential of being an invaluable tool for the genealogist, they have their drawbacks too. Broadsides are not easy to date. If the date is not on the broadside itself, the print and paper can not be used to indicate the approximate date of issue. Some Civil War ballads were produced on field presses in military camps during lulls in the fighting. Many items were printed in small editions and given away free. Since at the time most were not considered worth keeping, and preserving those that were kept was difficult; many broadsides did not survive.

Several private collections were established because of a combination of patriotism and potential profit. But others are where researchers can use them. The Massachusetts Historical Society has a large number of original and photographed copies of broadsides, as do a number of other state historical societies. Major university libraries; such as Oxford, Harvard, Brown, Emory, Duke, and Yale; also have broadsides in their archives. Broadsides can be found in a variety of other places; such as the boston, Houston, and Enoch Pratt Free Libraries; the Essex Institute; the Confederate Museum, the Library of Congress; and the London Public Record Office.

Unfortunately few small libraries, even if they own broadsides, have them catalogued. So they would not show up in the average card catalog. And going through the library's "pile" of broadsides for specific ones mentioning particular families would be time-consuming and probably fruitless. Because of the lack of cataloguing and understanding, broadsides are a grossly underused genealogy tool.

For those libraries, the local historical and genealogical societies can be of great help by offering to separate and sort their broadsides.

I've only to pick up
a newspaper and I seem
to see ghosts gliding
between the lines.
    -Henrik Ibsen
        Ghosts

15

Newspaper Morgue

Although early Romans imparted news with scrolls before Christ's birth, crude newspapers did not really begin until the early 1600's. And they were broadsides.

The first regularly published newspaper in what would become the United States was the weekly *Boston News-Letter* begun in 1704. Among stories of genealogical interest that first year of publication was the story of the taking of a sloop by pirates. "Captain Larew was kill'd and 20 of his men kill'd and wounded." The captain's descendants would find that of interest. In addition, even the advertisements had potential genealogical evidence. In the same issue the publisher announced that ads would be open to
"All Persons who have any Houses, Lands, Tenements, Farmes, Ships Vessels, Goods Wares or Merchandizes, Etc., to be Sold or Lett; or Servants Runaway or Goods Stoll or Lost, may have the same Inserted at a Reasonable Rate; from Twelve Pense to Five Shillings..."
Want ads for any of these items could have provided a researcher with more clues of where to continue to look for genealogical material.

Each of those early newspaper catered to a specific readership, be it a community, a nationality, or religious group. In 1866, even Russian-owned Alaska had a pen-and-ink newspaper in Point Clarence north of Nome. In 1884 Germans published 621 of the 794 immigrant/foreign language presses in the United States. But at the same time, the remaining 173 publications were published in Bohemian, French, Dutch, Hungarian, Italian, Polish, Scandinavian, Spanish and Welsh publications.

Family researchers might find information in any of these newspapers, including *The Jewish Courier*, a Yiddish paper from Chicago which advertized "Rabbi Leon Yaffee, Expert Circumcizer" and an Italian paper from New York which advertized

Fannie Horovitz
Italian Lawyer
Civil and Criminal Cases
299 Broadway, New York   Tel. Worth 5508

Although Fannie's Italian ancestry might come into question, the advertisement would still make interesting reading for present day Horovitz's.

Before the Trail of Tears, when the Indians were forced west; Chickasaws, Choctaws, Cherokees, Creeks and Seminoles were a highly educated group with teachers, tradesmen and plantation owners among their number. *The Cherokee Phoenix* became the first Indian newspaper. After the Trail of Tears a number of publications; including the *Indian Journal*, *The Cherokee Messenger*, *The Choctaw Telegraph* and *The Chickasaw and Choctaw Herald*; recorded the lives of the Indians in their new environment. Since Indian ancestry has been particularly difficult to trace, these publications have become even more important to the family historian.

Whether foreign, Indian or other, the newspaper is an important part of that community's identity. And the older newspapers of a community show the heritage of the group or area as it is directly linked to the group or area's present condition.

Despite the potential for information, newspapers have consistently been avoided by genealogists for several reasons. Usually a number of newspapers were published in each area over various time periods. In order to find the name of the newspaper which might benefit you, check county histories for the names of newspapers and the time frame of their publication. The public library is also a good source for this type of information.

Most newspapers keep copies of back issues in what they call their "morgues". Copies of defunct newspapers might be found in state or public libraries, historical societies, county courthouses, museums, or state or university archives.

Probably the most common reason for avoidance is that newspapers are not indexed. But there are several ways of checking newspapers without having to go through the each edition of the paper page by page for the entire time-period

your family was in the area. Libraries, genealogists or local genealogical societies sometimes have put together
- Obituaries, or some other specific sections of the paper, into indexed notebooks,
- Files of news articles, collected through the years, also frequently indexed,
- Books of articles from a specific time period.

If any of these types of projects have been done, the end result should be available in the local library. And sometimes the books of news articles are considered of wide enough interest to be published by a national publishing company like Genealogical Publishing Company's *Genealogical Data from Colonial New Haven Newspapers*.

The value of the American newspaper from the historical stand point can not be denied. Newspapers are also especially useful in discovering information about female ancestors who have been routinely left out of other genealogical sources. And probably the most useful pieces of information found in a newspaper are the vital statistics every genealogist searches for; such as birth, death, and marriage announcements.

Of course there are the usual BIRTH announcements which, in addition to the names of the baby and the parents, usually include the names of both sets of grandparents. But even if the grandparents are not listed, the baby's name might lead somewhere. For instance, James Dodd McKee may have had a Dodd in his ancestry.

While the August 12, 1904 OBITUARY of Mrs. A.H. Ames only told the reader that she died the previous Wednesday, leaving a husband and small children; other obituaries gave much more information. For instance, a Connecticut newspaper reported that Rev. Marston Cabot of Thompson died after a "day of fasting and prayer" in 1756. That same year, Joseph Fox of Glassenbury "when splitting posts, accidentally cut off one of his legs and died a few hours later."

Illness also was considered newsworthy. An October 30, 1903 article reported that
"Mr. Jas. H. Smith was continued to his room this week with fever but is out again."

In the SOCIAL section of the newspaper, a local resident would write about illnesses, visitors, anniversaries, reunions, achievements, newcomers, and other news of a more personal nature.

And sometimes even death intruded into the social news.
For instance, an *East Mississippi Times* reported that
> "Mrs. Jim McGee, who has been visiting her mother, Mrs.
> Reese, was called home Wednesday, to Okolona on account
> of the sudden death of her father-in-law."

Visitations were big news in small towns and their
reports contained impressive amounts of genealogical
information. For instance,
> "Mrs. J.R. Storment visited her daughter, Mrs. French, at
> West Point Sunday,"
revealed to the researcher that one of the Storment daughters
married someone named French and moved to West Point, giving
the researcher another name and another town in which to look
of data. It also told the researcher that both Mrs. Storment
and Mrs. French were still alive at the time of the article.

Likewise, the news article relating that
> "Miss Lorena Rushing left Saturday last to spend a few
> weeks with her sister, Mrs. Tyndall of Houston"
provided a Rushing researcher a great deal of information in
such a short space. Another article advised that Mr. R.B.
Neal, who was
> "engaged on the construction of the new railroad between
> Okolona and Houston spent last Wednesday with his
> family."
And, finally,
> "Mrs. J.P. Castles celebrated her birthday anniversary
> Friday by having a few of her lady friends and her sister
> Mrs. M.A. McKnight and family with her,"
contributed Mrs. Castles' husband's name, her sister's married
name, and her birth date to a researcher's knowledge.

Parties that were reported in the newspaper were
frequently full of pertinent information for the family
historian. Just think of all the information a researcher
found in an article about the WEDDING reception for Mr. and
Mrs. Clyde Taylor Travis in the home of the brides parents,
Mr. and Mrs. R.E. Williams. Listed in the article were members
of the bridal party and out-of-town guests which included
obvious family members and the towns in which they lived.

The 1906 newspaper coverage of the double wedding of
Robert Hunter to Miss R.D. Neal and William Homes Sikes to
Miss Bessie Neal includes -
> "Mrs. W.D. Hartness and Miss Willie Neal, sisters of the
> brides were matron and maid of honor, and Messers John
> Neal and Elno Davis were attendants of the groom. The
> ushers, Misses Mary Bell Sikes, Susie Harrington, Hadye

Critz and Mollie Funderburk preceeded the bridal party to the alter..."
giving the family genealogist an extraordinary amount of information. For instance, researchers of the Sikes family learn that William Homes Sikes probably had a sister named Mary Bell and that his wife Bessie had sisters named R.D., Mrs. W.D. Hartness, and Willie and probably a brother named John.

The news article about the wedding of Annie McArn to Thomas McKell, son of Isabella McKell gave more information about the family's history than the average wedding coverage.
"A June wedding, beautiful in its simplicity was solemized in the parlors of the bride's home... On account of a late bereavement in the family, the death less than a year ago, of the mother, only immediate family and a few close friends were invited... The bride is the daughter of Mr. John McArn, one of the prominent planters of that section, and a neice of the late Col. J.L. Power, Secretary of State."

SCHOOL news might have detailed coverage of high school or eighth grade graduation, including class names and pictures; lists of teachers; and participants in a school play.

News about CLUB and ORGANIZATION meetings might have given names of members of fraternal organizations, political groups and public safety (fire and police) associations; all of which lead to more places to search.

Normal LOCAL NEWS articles also might have contained a great deal of information for the genealogist who knows how to find it. Whether the story is about the fire in the home of widow Willard of Newington, Connecticut in 1769; or about the residents of the poorhouse in a Georgia town, an ancestor might be discovered.

You never know what you might learn about your ancestors from those local news items in old papers. Articles from an 1833 *New York Sun* included one about the suicide of Fred A. Hall, a boarder at Webb's Congress Hall. According to the newspaper account
"He was to have sailed yesterday morning for Sumatra, as supercargo of a vessel belonging to ... his father. He is supposed to have committed this rash act in a temporary derangement occasioned by an affair of the heart in which his happiness was deeply involved."

PUBLIC NOTICES might have included lists of officials of county and city government and ministers of area churches. At times, lists of the tax rolls, property to be sold for taxes and even slaves to be sold at auction have appeared in newspapers. Ancestor Ed Buckner, county assessor in 1904, might have placed a notice in the newspaper that the Tax Roll was on file at the Chancery Clerk's office. Or. S.J. Wallace, superintendent of schools, might have announced that ancestor Hugh Critz was the new member of the Board of School Examiners. As with many other newspapers, in 1761, a local Middletown, Connecticut newspaper published a list of all of those with unclaimed letters in the post office.

Under the heading "Police Office" in an 1833 New York newspaper appeared the story of
"John Evans, brought up for throwing stones at the house of Eliza Vincent."
The story would be of unusual interest to descendants of John Evans, especially if he had eventually married Eliza.

And what might McMan/McMann descendants think of the "Police Office" account of their ancestor John McMan who was
"brought up for whipping Juda McMan, his darling wife - his excuse was, that his head was rather thick, in consequence of taking a wee drab of whiskey. Not being able to find bail he was accommodated with a room in (jail)."
or Reed descendants reading the March 31, 1875 *Romeo Observer* that reported
"Yesterday John Haber who lives a mile south and three-fourths of a mile east of Romeo, procured the arrest of a Mrs. Reed for assault and battery with intent to take a scalp."
And on November 2, 1870, the same paper reported that
"Charles Wilcox who is employed at A.J. Parker's restaurant, in a scuffle with Dr. T. W. Stitt, was thrown in such a way to have his left leg broken just above the ankle. He is improving."

And finally, descendants might find interesting the article in an 1833 New York paper which told of William Scott of Centre Market, who was arrested for
"assaulting Charlotte Gray, a young woman with whom he lived."
When the magistrate discovered the couple had never married, he gave Scott the choice of prison or marrying Gray.
"Mr. Scott cast a sheeps eye towards the girl, and then looking out of the window, gave (the jail) a melancholy survey; he then gave the girl another look, and was hesitating as to which he should choose - a wife or a

prison. The Justice insisted on an immediate answer. At
length he included what he 'might as well marry the
critter' and they left the office apparently satisfied."

As a genealogical source, a Mississippi ADVERTISEMENT for
the Carpenter Grocery Company's Going-Out-Of-Business Sale
imparted some information to a Carpenter researcher. A
People's Bank ad mentioned that W.W. Scales was president,
M.F. Ames was vice-president, and A.C. Ervin was cashier. And
a Wofford researcher might have been interested to learn that
A.A. Wofford was a dentist whose office was in the "Opera
House over Caldwell and Lampkin's stores."

In Romeo, Michigan, a December 15, 1869 advertisement
appeared as a news article reporting that
"Hiram J. Mann commenced an omnibus to and from the
depot, on last Monday. He attends to all orers for
passengers to any part of the village, and always arrives
at the depot in time for all trains."
In addition to learning that Mann ran a taxi service in Romeo,
if there has been any question, his descendant can place Mann
as an adult in Romeo in 1869.

Some valuable advertisements even appeared on the front
page in those early days. In a Cheyenne, Wyoming paper, E.A.
Reed managed to get his Wyoming Furniture and Undertaker
Company in the front page ad. Portland's *Daily Eastern Argus*
advertised Wright's Indian Vegetable Pills which the ad
claimed cured "all billous complaints."

If a town was too small to have its own newspaper, there
still might have been a section for news from the area in a
neighboring larger town's newspaper. Most county seat
newspapers included information about families in OUTLYING
AREAS.

But even if your family has never appeared in the
newspaper, studying advertisements in the paper gives a look
at the fashions, goods and costs; and examining articles lets
you understand the conditions in the community at the time
your ancestor was there.

Articles in the old newspaper might be written a little
more flowery than you are used to. A fire might become a
"conflagration". An answer might become a "rejoinder." But if
you can get past the verbose style, you just might find the
material you need to continue your search.

16

Time After Time

English and American birth, death and marriage dates
prior to 1751 can be very confusing. Numerous calendar changes
have made the dating system probably one of the most difficult
things for a researcher to understand. But as a researcher,
you need to understand calendar changes that have taken place
in order to be sure that the dates with which you are working
are the correct ones.

The problem has been going on since long before Christ.
In 45 B.C. Julius Caesar's JULIAN Calendar attempted to
correct earlier calendar errors by assigning one additional
(leap) day to every fourth year. But by studying the
equinoxes, it became evident that, in reality, the error had
required an adding of only 7 days every 900 years rather than
25 days every 100 years. So more corrections were needed.

In an attempt to off-set the Julian Calendar's over-
correction, another calendar which omitted ten days beginning
on October 4th, 1582, was released during Pope Gregory XIII's
reign. So the next day; October 5th, 1582; became October
15th. Even though Roman Catholic nations adopted the new
calendar immediately, England and the other Protestant nations
did not adopt the GREGORIAN Calendar until 1752. Because of
the delay, by the time Protestant countries finally adopted
the calendar, eleven rather than ten days had to be skipped.
And so, September 3rd, 1752 became September 14th.

English legislation that required the omission of those
eleven days, also shortened the previous year. Prior to that

time, the new year began on March 25th. But because of the legislation, 1752 began with what would have been on January 1, 1751 instead of March 25, 1752. So when an event took place in a Protestant country in a January, February or March prior to 1752, the double-year date (i.e. February 3, 1682/3) has usually been used in books to indicate both the old and new calendar.

To figure a date before 1752, eleven days need to be subtracted and, for events occurring between January 1 and March 25, one year needs to be subtracted. Something that occurred on January 21, 1740 under the old calendar, would be dated January 10, 1741 under the new one.

French, Italian or Spanish birth, death or marriage dates on original records prior to October 4, 1582, would have been given using the old style calendar. Similarly, English, Scottish or American dates prior to January 1, 1751 would have used the old style.

When using dates in books and newspapers from before the adoption of the Gregorian calendar, it is important to know if the date was from the ecclesiastical, legal or calendar year. And the researcher needs to know if the author/editor of the book has already translated the old style to the new; or if the dates given were as they appeared in the original document.

For the laborer is
worthy of his hire.
-7 St. Luke
Bible

17

Five W's and a "How" of
Hiring a Professional Genealogist

I have frequently wondered WHY people hire me, spend
perfectly good money, to do searches when so much of the
information they need can be obtained by writing a query to
the appropriate public library. There is so much that can be
done by an organized individual, just using the U.S. Postal
Service.

But in some cases there are advantages to hiring a
genealogist. The professional can work faster strictly because
of their familiarity with the area and their knowledge of
WHERE to go for the information. A professional genealogist
would know where the cemeteries are, that old newspapers are
stored in the basement of the courthouse, and that the county
historical museum is only open from 1:00 to 4:00 p.m. on
Tuesday, Wednesday and Thursday.

For that reason, it is important to hire a genealogist as
close as possible to the area you want searched. In addition
to faster retrieval of the information, mileage costs can be
kept down.

But WHEN should you hire a professional? If you have
tried every avenue you can think of, if you have enough
information to know without a doubt that you are on the right
track, and if hiring a professional would be a lot less
expensive then going to the area yourself; you should consider
hiring a genealogist.

However, if you have been searching for your ancestors by
yourself and have not found the information you need, then the
evidence you are seeking might just not be available - not
even to a professional.

In addition, a professional provides a clear head, a fresh view at looking at the information available. Perhaps you have missed something. One amateur researcher did not realize that the James Allen who married Jemema C. Collier on March 16, 1842 in Itawamba County, Mississippi, as recorded by one author; was the same as James Allen who married Jemema Dollar in March, 1842 in Itawamba. The Collier and Dollar names looked, when written, and sounded, when spoken, very similar.

If you have finally decided to hire a genealogist the next step is to decide WHO to hire. Genealogical Certification has been around since 1964 when the Board of Certification of Genealogists (BCG) was established to administer qualifying exams and maintain a register of certified person. After qualifying, a professional can use the initials after his name of the category he has qualified for - Certified Genealogical Record Searcher (C.G.R.S.), American Lineage Specialist (C.A.L.S.), American Indian Lineage Specialist (C.A.I.L.S.), Genealogist (C.G.), Genealogical Lecturer (C.G.L.) or Genealogical Instructor (C.G.I.). The cost to become certified in well in excess of $100.

The BCG does no genealogical research itself. Nor does it guarantee the work of anyone it certifies. However, if the BCG receives complaints, it will investigate and, if the complaints prove valid, the BCG will de-certify the offender.

There are several other certification programs. For instance, the Mormons have their own accreditation program.

The Association of Professional Genealogists was formed in 1979 to promote professionalism in genealogy. It produces a quarterly journal and a biennial directory of professional genealogists. They also maintain a professional committee which will confidentially arbitrate differences between clients and the professional. The cost of membership is $35 a year.

A certified genealogist is generally more experienced and more expensive then an uncertified one, but not always. Many genealogists who do searches in rural areas tend to not become certified strictly because of the cost involved. They do not get enough business, or earn enought income to justify the cost. However, they know their locality as well as any certified genealogist might.

Whether certified or not, a professional, in addition to researching individual families, may also lecture, publish, develop software and even testify in legal cases. Some form cooperatives and work with other professionals in the region.

But HOW do you know a good genealogist from a bad one? Expect professionals to send you a resume, listing their education, publications, and professional affiliations. Make sure those credentials match your special needs. Are you looking for someone to write up your family in book form? Then you need to make sure your professional has writing skills.

If you are still not sure if you want to hire a specific researcher, ask for and check out references. Did other clients feel they got their money's worth?

But remember, rates vary depending on the region, competition and experience of the researcher. So you can not determine the quality of the work which will be done by the price which is quoted. Most professionals charge by the hour, with additional charges for travel, photocopying and postage. Some researchers include mileage in their hourly rates. Others charge separate hourly and mileage rates. With the price of gas what it is, mileage costs have gone quite high. But whatever the cost, the price per mile should not be any higher than the U.S. government allows as an income tax business deduction. Most researchers require a deposit which is then applied to the final bill.

Cost can't help but be a big consideration for most people. While the cost covers the time spent, it does not insure success. A competent researcher can spend hours going through courthouse records and never find the name for which they are searching.

In Mississippi, most counties did not begin to record births and deaths until the late 1800's or later. Courthouses fires were frequent. A family could have rented a home in a Mississippi county and never have shown up in any record in the courthouse.

Once you have decided upon your researcher, you need to present the material you have collected in the best way so that the professional does not waste his time and your money going over old ground.

Be concise. You are so familiar with the material you have, it makes sense to you. But read through the information you are sending with an open mind. Will your professional understand what you are writing without having to read through it three or four times?

Likewise, if you send copies of everything you have concerning the family, you will end up paying for the genealogist sifting through it. Give only pertinent, well-organized information.

A professional genealogist wants only facts, your guesses might lead a genealogist in the wrong direction. Let your genealogist know when something is a guess or an estimate. You might be tempted to tell a librarian, whose services are free, that you are sure your ancestor came from her town when you haven't the foggiest idea where the ancestor was from. But it is just plain dumb to feed that nonsense to a genealogist you are paying.

One client had read a name on a handwritten early marriage record as Serena Davis. So that was the name she wanted researched. When Serena Davis could not be found, the professional asked her client to send a photocopy of the marriage licence. It was obvious to the professional that the name was Jemima David. The client had guessed at what the handwritten record had said. "Per hour" means just that and that particular client wasted a lot of money because she sent the professional incorrect information. So be as accurate as possible with names, dates and places.

Be clear about what information you want and why you want it. Do you want information only about your direct ancestor? Or do you want all the information your professional can find about the entire family - brothers and sisters, nephews and nieces, aunts and uncles of your ancestor? Lineage society applications frequently require photocopies or certified copies of original documents. Is that what you need or will a summary of the information be acceptable?

Give your researcher an idea of how much you are willing to spend. As can be seen below, fees for even a relatively inexpensive researcher can add up fast.

5 hours research at $15 per hour	$ 75.00
2 hours report preparation at $15 per hour	30.00
30 miles at 25 cents per mile	7.50
Postage	1.25
Plat map	2.00
10 copies at courthouse at 50 cents per copy	5.00
10 copies at library at 25 cents per copy	2.50
	$123.25

If you ask a professional to drive one hundred miles to get a copy of a marriage record, it could cost you between $30 and $50. But a letter to the courthouse or department of vital statistics could get you a copy for $10.

If you want cemetery records checked for your family, hiring a genealogist from the area in which your ancestors were buried could cost anywhere from $15 to $75. But if you write the public library in that area and ask the librarians to photocopy the appropriate pages, it will probably cost between $2 and $5 in copying and postage charges.

It's your choice.

Tormenting the
people with trivia
—Napoleon I
*Memoirs...
ecrits a Ste.
Helene*

18

Leftovers

Unusual MEASUREMENTS sometime show up in records. Some you might run into are found below.

An "arpent" and a "perche" are French linear measurements used in older documents.

1 arpent = 1.5 acres
27.5 arpents = 1 U.S. mile
1 perche = 19.188 feet

Other measurements might not be foreign, but might still be unfamiliar. In measurements of surface

1 hectare = 10,000 square meters or 2.471 acres

Occasionally apothecary weights and terms show up in literature. They translate to

20 grains = 1 scruple
3 scruples = 1 drachm

And, of course, there is the measurement that all Americans really should know, but seldom do. That is

1 kilometer = .62137 miles

In the New World there was an abundance of different currencies. States issued their own MONEY which frequently crossed state and even national borders. Much of the different monies circulated at varying rates of discount. In the late 1830's, Alabama money was considered the best in Mississippi even though Mississippi produced its own money. The majority of the Mississippi money was circulated by a bank in Brandon. However, other banks in Mississippi were also given the right to issue money.

The United States was not the only place with the multiple currencies. In 1793, approximately four hundred institutions were issuing notes in England. Unification of Germany did not take place until late in the 1800's. In Prussia, alone, there were ten provinces during the 19th century. Then for several decades after World War II, Germany was divided again. When Germany was not unified, each segment produced its own money.

In the Old Northwest Territory of North America, monies from four countries were used. Halifax currency was worth less than British Sterling. New York was worth less than Halifax. In 1780, John Askin related that

Halifax currency = 75-80% Sterling
New York currency = 60% Halifax

At the same time, a livre, a French unit of currency, was also being accepted and

1 livre = 1 pound of silver

Family researchers sometimes forget that in addition to entering the United States, their ancestors were also quite capable of leaving the country. And while recent PASSPORT applications can easily be found, older versions are also available. At one time, passports were needed to go to Michigan, Florida, the Mississippi Valley, and farther west. But those were the times when the areas were not part of the United States: they were French, Spanish, British or Indian territories.

Before 1824, the Secretary of War was responsible for relations with Indians, including the issuance of passports into their territory. An example of one such passport which contained a great deal of data for a family historian read

"Thomas Crittondon, Jeremiah Day & John Austin with their families consisting of twenty two persons on Board a flat Bottomed Boat, have permission to descend the River Tennessee & the other waters lying in their way to Natchez, they conducting with propriety & conforming to the Laws & regulations adopted to the Government of the Indian Department."

The entry was signed by J. Meigs and dated May 22, 1803.

In the 18th and early 19th centuries, the French and then the British controlled the Old Northwest Territory. Instead of passports, notarized contracts were used by voyagers going into that area and down the Mississippi River. Most of these travelers were the hardy bunch of steersmen and oarsmen from fur traders' canoes. One July, 1816 entry reported that

Etienne Lamoiandiere contracted Antoine Leduc to travel to Chicago.

Many of those contracts can be found in the Michilimackinac Notary Public Book in Bayliss Library in Sault Ste. Marie, Michigan.

The one problem with university records is that some, such as transcripts, are kept closed during a person's life. And frequently after the person's death, the only way a researcher can get them released is with the permission of the executor of the estate or a court order. At a minimum, a death certificate may be needed.

A lot of critical sources - both books and records - are in other languages. Invest in a good FOREIGN LANGUAGE dictionary.

America did not have its own paper mill until 1816 and Jefferson wrote with a quill pen. Old inks frequently evaporated or the vegetable matter in it decayed.

Only recently have spellings of words been standardized. Before that, spellings varied between writers and documents. Add to the problem the trouble of trying to decipher the handwriting and reading old documents becomes extremely difficult.

The letter "s" probably causes more trouble than any other when deciphering handwriting. "Ross" can look like "Roofs," "Roops," or "Rofs." "Esther" can look like "Efther."

Kirkham's *The Handwriting of American Records for a Period of 300 Years* is an superb handbook for deciphering early documents. Kirkham even displays samples of handwriting idiosyncracies from other countries.

19

Putting It All Together

First, regard all family tales of coats of arms and royal lineage with skepticism. Just because there is a Seymore family crest, it doesn't mean your Seymores have one. And if you do find you are descended from King Henry I of England, it will be far more likely to be through one of his more than 20 illegitimate children.

Whatever information you find, WRITE IT DOWN. You might not see a connection at the time, but you might when you get a chance to sit down and truly study it, or even later, when you have collected more evidence.

Family record books, whether handmade or purchased from a local bookstore or stationers, make valued gifts for children and grandchildren. Pictures tell their own stories, so you might like to include any you find of ancestors. Be sure to mention heirlooms and traditions that have been passed through the family and anecdotes you uncover about individuals.

Store old documents away from light, heat and humidity. Mold and mildew can eat away documents. Temperatures should remain stable - no hotter than 72 degrees. Basements and attics are the worse possible places to store old documents but are commonly where those same documents are uncovered.

Documents should be kept in acid-free folders or envelopes and filed in acid-free boxes. Scrapbooks and photographic albums can also be purchased with acid-free pages.

We all know something about our living relatives and enjoy recalling their achievements and exploits. And we are certainly fond of those characters that most families have.

But how many of us have been able to know our great-grandparents? Much of what we are today is because of what they wanted out of life, why they immigrated to the U.S., how they raised their children and how they lived their lives.

A family record is not just names, dates and places. It concerns people - what they did, why and how. As Steven Vincent Benet wrote,

"There were human beings aboard the Mayflower, not merely ancestors".